Mary Elizabeth Braddon

Hostages to fortune

Vol. II

Mary Elizabeth Braddon

Hostages to fortune
Vol. II

ISBN/EAN: 9783337050597

Printed in Europe, USA, Canada, Australia, Japan

Cover: Foto ©ninafisch / pixelio.de

More available books at **www.hansebooks.com**

HOSTAGES TO FORTUNE

LONDON:
ROBSON AND SONS, PRINTERS, PANCRAS ROAD, N.W.

HOSTAGES TO FORTUNE

A Novel

BY THE AUTHOR OF

'LADY AUDLEY'S SECRET'

ETC. ETC. ETC.

IN THREE VOLUMES

VOL. II.

LONDON
JOHN MAXWELL AND CO.
4 SHOE LANE, FLEET STREET
1875
[All rights reserved]

HOSTAGES TO FORTUNE

CHAPTER I.

'We can be nothing to each other, and yet are too much to each other. . . . . I will see thee no more. All I can say is mere folly. In future I shall see thee as men see the stars.'

HERMAN is not false to his promise made at the railway-station. He works as he has seldom worked before; labours for long hours with a spring and a freshness in his work that make it light. Bright thoughts come to him unsought; the gold lies on the surface. It is as if some fairy sat beside him and breathed happy fancies into his mind. There is no grinding against the grain. His pen, swift as habit has made it, cannot keep pace with his fancy. And he knows that this new book—higher in design, simpler in treatment than any other story of his—

will be popular, let the *Censor* pronounce what judgment it may. The characters which have such a vigorous life for him will live for his readers. In his last effort there might have been too much labour, a studied simplicity, a too elaborate puritanism. In this story Fancy follows her own wayward will, Imagination is dominant over Art.

Herman has not availed himself of Mr. Lyndhurst's invitation for the Derby, Editha being in town at the time of the Epsom saturnalia, and all the races that were ever run being of no more account to her lover than a race of flies across the ceiling.

Dropping into the greenroom of the Frivolity one evening to discuss certain vague ideas for a new comedy with Myra—he never goes to her house now—Herman finds Mr. Lyndhurst leaning in his favourite attitude against the mantelpiece, talking to Miss Walters, the soubrette, who in the matter of slang is more than a match for him.

'Rather unfriendly of you to throw me over the other day, Westray,' says Mr. Lyndhurst, as they shake hands, while Miss Walters withdraws to the other end of the room, and contemplates her blue-satin hessians in the glass.

'It really wasn't an engagement, you know. I told you I was likely to be engaged elsewhere.'

'Did you? I thought you were booked for my party. We had rather a jolly day. Earlswood was with us, and so-and-so, and so-and-so,' running over a string of names; 'just the right people for that kind of thing; and we wound up with a dinner at the Pandemos. However, perhaps our party on Thursday will be more in your line; small and select—Mrs. Brandreth and Earlswood, Miss Belormond and myself. Just room for you. We're going to post down. Will you come?'

Herman Westray hesitates. Hamilton Lyndhurst is of all men the one whose acquaintance he cares least to cultivate just now—the man he would least like to see a frequent guest in that home which is now his daydream. But he and Lyndhurst have been on friendly terms for the last five years; he has cultivated the man's society at odd times, regarding him as an interesting specimen amid the varieties of mankind; and, whatever his views for the future, he cannot well be uncivil to Mr. Lyndhurst in the present.

While he pauses, undecided, Mrs. Brandreth comes in, flushed and breathless after a powerful piece of declamation at the end of an act. The withdrawal of *Hemlock* has been followed by an adaptation of a play by Dumas, which has startled all Paris at the Gymnase; but which, with its motive cut clean away and its morality whitewashed, has been tortured into an invertebrate domestic drama, and has signally failed in its attempt to startle London. This piece having been unlucky—though prepared by an eminent hand—Mrs. Brandreth is desperately anxious to get a play from Herman.

'I have been asking Westray to join our party on Thursday,' says Lyndhurst.

'And he has said yes, I hope,' exclaims Myra. 'How nice that will be! We can discuss your ideas for the new piece,' she adds, turning radiantly to Herman.

'It will be against the interests of the new piece that I should take a day's holiday. I am working very closely just now.'

'All the more reason that you should allow yourself a few hours' respite,' says Myra.

Herman is doubtful. Those double tides have kept him close to his desk, and he has a very human desire for fresh air and sunshine, the lights and shadows on a breezy heath, the concourse of prosperous well-dressed mankind, a race on which fortunes are won and lost. The racing year is getting old, and he has not seen one of the horses he hears men talk about at his club.

'If I could spare the day,' he says, wavering.

'If you can! Why, you will work all the better afterwards!'

'I fear not. There must be something mechanical in my workmanship; for throw me out of gear, and it takes ever so long before the wheels go again. I am like one of those monster ironworks one reads of in the North, where it takes a week to get the fires lighted.'

'Bank up your fires on Wednesday night, and you'll be ready for a vigorous start on Friday morning,' says Lyndhurst. 'If you are a mechanical writer, you should go to work like your brother-novelist Philpott, who writes eight folios every morning, neither more nor less, and leaves off at a hyphen rather than begin a ninth. That's the way to write novels.'

'Do go,' pleads Myra; and something in her tone brings back the old days when the lightest word from her would have been a command—that one happy summer time when her beauty and genius brightened the little world of home. She seems ten years younger to him just in this moment. Only for one moment. In the next the consciousness of all that has come and gone since those days flashes back upon him. Life is full of these brief waking trances—this catalepsy of memory.

'What can you want with me?' he asks. 'You cannot have a more amusing companion than Lyndhurst, and Lord Earlswood is to be with you.'

'I want to talk to you about a new piece. This *Hands, not Hearts,* is an abominable failure, although Paris is raving about it. I suppose it only proves the difference between Fargueil's power and mine.'

'I think it only proves that when you take away

the motive of a play, and alter the relations of the principal characters towards each other, you weaken it considerably; to say nothing of the discount to be allowed for the change from the brightest and most epigrammatic of languages to our lumpish Saxon.'

'You'll come on Thursday?'

'Of course, if you make a point of it. I have rather a good idea for the end of the second act which I should like to talk over with you. I know your tact in the arrangement of situation. You'll be sure to give me some valuable hints.'

His belief in her talent is unbounded. This unlucky adaptation has given new and striking proof of her power. She has borne the weight of the piece on her shoulders, and the scenes in which she appears have gone brilliantly, although the play has failed to draw money. It has been *un succès d'actrice*.

The Cup-day opens brilliantly—Queen's weather, as all the newspapers exclaim in chorus, dimly reminiscent of the day when Majesty adorned the Berkshire racecourse.

Herman feels that this brief pause in his busy life is worth having. Summer is so sweet a thing in this early stage, with all her freshness upon her, before the fruit has begun to ripen on old garden walls, before the scythe has slain the glory of long feathery grasses, or the song of nightingale has died in the twilit woodland.

Mr. Lyndhurst picks Mr. Westray up at his chambers at eleven o'clock, the last of the party. Mrs. Brandreth and Miss Belormond are in the capacious landau; Lord Earlswood and his confidential groom occupy the box; a basket swings behind; four horses and two blue-jacketed postillions astonish the bystanders.

Myra looks charming in a toilette which is of the simplest, yet has a picturesque grace that might do credit to Worth himself. The fabric of the dress is creamy-hued cambric, disposed in manifold plaitings; its only embellishment a broad sash of palest azure and a sprinkling of pale azure bows, like a flight of heaven-coloured butterflies. A soft cream-coloured felt hat—after Vandyke—with a long azure feather and massive silver buckle, completes Mrs.

Brandreth's costume. Miss Belormond's brilliant mauve and white costume has cost three times as much; but Miss Belormond at best resembles an animated fashion-plate, while Myra looks as if she had stepped out of an old picture.

Miss Belormond is a young lady who has devoted herself to the drama chiefly because she is handsome, and is expected to make her mark speedily as the beautiful Miss Belormond; secondly, because she and her immediate friends imagine that what Mrs. Brandreth has done may be as easily achieved by any young woman of equal personal attractions. And Miss Belormond is much handsomer than Mrs. Brandreth. Her eyes are larger, her complexion finer, her mouth more nearly resembles Cupid's bow, her figure is infinitely superior to Myra's, which has little to recommend it except consummate grace. In a word, then, Miss Belormond's friends come to the conclusion that the young lady has nothing to do but go in and win. Love of dramatic art—liking even—she has none; she has never recited six lines of Shakespeare voluntarily in her life, or been moved by a play. But she can be taught, argue her friends; it is all an affair of tuition; and as Miss Belormond has discovered all at once that she is dying to make her *début* as Juliet in white satin and silver passementerie, she is eager to learn. So she is handed over to one of the dramatic grinders, and is taught the same tones, and turns of head and arm, and inflections and tremulosos, that have been ground into Miss Wilson and Miss Milson, Miss Stokes and Miss Nokes, and in due course turned out of hand a finished Juliet. Her parents are not wealthy enough to defray the charges of this training, or to supply the costly raiment in which Miss Belormond thinks it indispensable to appear at rehearsal, nor are they influential enough to procure that *début* for which the young lady pines; but she is happily endowed with a rich godfather, who seems to be a near relation of Cinderella's fairy sponsor, and this gentleman—gray-moustached and in the sugar-baking trade—kindly arranges everything, even to the neat single brougham which is indispensable to Miss Belormond's launch—without which, indeed, that trim-built vessel could scarcely be got off the stocks.

Bella Walters and the unbelieving of the Frivolity corps have wondered not a little that Mrs. Brandreth should engage so handsome a woman as 'Belormond' to act with her; but to see the two together is to find the answer to the enigma. That handsome dolt, splendid in colouring, perfect in feature, but with no more soul or spontaneous vitality than if she had been made by Madame Tussaud, is the best foil that the electrical Myra could have devised for herself. The expressionless beauty of this dull creature gives point and piquancy to Myra's countenance, which is all expression. The lifeless perfection of one enhances the charm of the other, and Myra is never so enchanting as when her imperfections are contrasted with this faultless nullity.

The two women have not a thought in common, Miss Belormond's mind seldom soaring above the contemplation of a new dress or the expectation of a little dinner. They rarely meet outside the theatre, and Miss Belormond's experiences at rehearsal have inspired a wholesome fear of her manageress. Myra's polished sarcasms sting her like the cut of a lash, and she has more than once hinted to the fairy godfather that she will never know real bliss until she has a theatre of her own, and actresses of her own to sneer at, as Mrs. Brandreth sneers at her—remarks which the fairy godfather allows to pass him by like the idle wind.

Miss Belormond therefore, aware that this companionship of to-day is a condescension on Mrs. Brandreth's part, is on her best behaviour, and is for the most part content to simper and say nothing. There is a drop of bitter mingled with her cup of sweetness, in the fact that she has accepted Mr. Lyndhurst's invitation without the consent or knowledge of that benevolent godfather; nay, that she has been guilty of overt deception in informing her estimable sponsor that she is going to spend the day with her aunt Drayson, at Nightingale-terrace, New-cross.

Mr. Lyndhurst is tired of the vapid beauty already, though he has not been a quarter of an hour in her society.

'I wish I'd asked Bella Walters,' he says to himself; 'there's more fun in that cock-nosed little puss than in a regiment of Belormonds.'

Herman, who has seen Miss Belormond about the theatre, and noticed her about as much as he would have noticed any other handsome piece of furniture, greets her politely, but wonders not a little what she and Myra do in the same galley, outside the theatre. He does not know that this business of to-day is one of love's many meannesses. Myra, who now so seldom sees him, lowers herself to doubtful company for the sake of being for a few hours with him. Had he refused Mr. Lyndhurst's invitation, she would have found an excuse for staying at home on the Cup-day.

He is here, and she is all life and brightness, ready to talk of anything or everything. There is a worldly flavour in her talk—a spice of lemon and cayenne—which is refreshing from its novelty. With Editha he has been always in the skies, her world not being his world, nor her thoughts his thoughts. Even in talking of literature Myra has the advantage over the well-read country maiden; for Myra reads only the books of the day—books whose titles are on all men's lips—and always contrives to read them while they are fresh. The last argumentative battering-ram brought to bear upon the citadel of Christian faith, the last French novel with its apotheosis of femine infidelity, are alike familiar to her. She can talk of the gravest themes or the lightest, and has something trenchant or sparkling to say of all.

Herman feels like a man who, after riding some quiet cob for a while, returns to the lively thorough-bred he rode before, and, as the pace increases, experiences a new sense of rapture and feels a forgotten power come back to him. This worldly talk is passing pleasant—pleasanter, perhaps, for the rattling pace of the carriage as it skims along the broad high-road, with its endless line of prim suburban villas, fringed with young limes and slim pink hawthorns and mop-shaped young trees of tenderest green, all after the same pattern; pleasanter, perhaps, because of the bright and varying face opposite him, smiling under the soft shadow of the Vandyke hat. Lyndhurst, tired of listening, tries to develop the conversational powers of Miss Belormond, who says, 'That they *do*,' and 'That he *does*,' when she is emphatically affirmative, and

'Not a bit of it' when negative. Earlswood sits on the box and converses with his groom, who has come to look after the postillions and make himself generally useful. His lordship is serious and meditative, as beseems a man whose losses or gains between this and sundown must be considerable.

'I hope I've done right in putting the pot on about Golden Fleece,' he says dubiously.

'Couldn't do better, my lord, after the information we had from—hum—hum—' replies the groom, dropping his voice to a confidential mumble.

They arrive on the heath just when the crowd is thickest, and before ascending to Mr. Lyndhurst's box, stroll up and down the lawn for a little, Herman and Mrs. Brandreth interchanging greetings with a good many people, Miss Belormond stared at freely, but not finding many of her acquaintance in these favoured regions.

Somehow—Herman can hardly tell how it has come about—Myra and he are more intimate to-day than they have ever been since their period of juvenile folly at Colehaven. He has given her his arm to steer her through the crowd, and the tapering hand, in a glove which in texture and colour resembles the petal of a tea-rose, rests confidingly upon his sleeve, so confidingly that he is fain to press it gently once or twice when the crowd is densest. Her talk is full of life and freshness— freshness as of Cliquot just uncorked rather than of forest rill. She criticises the people they pass, utters scathing cynicisms — borrowed from the *Scourge* or the *Censor*—with a delicious placidity, and contrives to interest her companion so completely that he is in no hurry to ascend to the box, whence Miss Belormond and Hamilton Lyndhurst are already raking the crowd with huge race-glasses. Earlswood is there too, and his smaller glass follows that pair below, with two angry eyes behind it.

Does Herman forget Editha on this sunlit Cup-day, amidst odours of Ess bouquet, and rustle of silk, and flutter of laces and muslins, and raucous cries of 'Ten to one on the field'? Well, no; his state of mind is hardly forgetfulness, but rather a calm severance from Editha and that portion of his life which belongs to her. He is a young man capable of leading two distinct lives—half a dozen distinct lives if they offered themselves to him with sufficient attractiveness—of playing Odysseus abroad or Odysseus at home as occasion served. If fate throw him into Circe's or Calypso's company, he will enjoy himself reasonably, but be not the less faithful to Penelope when he returns to the halls of Ithaca. He sees no harm in making himself pleasant to Myra to-day, especially after his categorical declaration of limited liability in the way of friendship. Of his engagement and approaching marriage he has said not a word; these are subjects too sacred to be talked about on race-courses or in greenrooms. The topics he discusses to-day are light as thistledown, and, like thistledown, float away and are forgotten. Yet perchance even this careless talk of to-day carries the germ of fertility with it, like that feathery seed, and will crop up somehow in days to come.

They go up to the box at last, where Miss Belormond, having stared at the women's dresses to satiety, is yawning behind her race-glass, and wondering whether the fairy godfather has quite accepted that fiction about aunt Drayson, and wishing that some one would propose an adjournment to lobster salad and moselle, or chicken sandwich and champagne.

This desired diversion comes almost immediately from Hamilton Lyndhurst, who is eager to escort the ladies to the refreshment-room, or to Mr. Vyne Hendler's private tent, where the initiated are being hospitably entertained all day long, and where royalty is supposed mostly to congregate.

Miss Belormond rises briskly at the first bidding, having retained her primitive simplicity in the matter of appetite. Mrs. Brandreth refuses to stir.

'Do you suppose I am going to allow myself to be trampled upon by a famishing crowd for the sake of a sandwich?' she asks. 'If you like to send me some claret-cup and a biscuit, I will take it here. Mr. Westray is going to tell me about his comedy.'

Miss Belormond departs on Hamilton's arm, with an awful feeling that the fairy godfather must hear of this somehow, and that her brougham and her silk dresses will be spirited away like Cinderella's finery at the stroke of twelve; but the present delight of being jostled in a well-dressed crowd, having sweet nothings murmured into her ear in Mr. Lyndhurst's legato baritone, and consuming lobster mayonnaise and champagne-cup—wholesome mixture!—outweigh that vague dread, and the fair Belormond, not having room in her brain for composite emotion, is happy. Lord Earlswood has gone down to talk to the bookmen, so Herman and Myra have the box to themselves. She sits with one arm resting listlessly upon the velvet cushion, her profile towards the crowd, and with about as much thought of the purpose of the meeting as if she had been at church. He sits with his back to the crowd and his chair tilted on its hind legs, thoughtful even to absent-mindedness.

'Do you remember the races at Tipsbury, the day papa drove us over in Mr. Sanderson's dog-cart?' asks Myra. 'What a delicious autumn day it was, and what lovely country—a stretch of common on the crest of a hill—and woods, woods, woods on every side, and the great blue sea shining at us through a break in the foliage! And what a simple-minded rustic meeting, half a race and half a fair! Do you remember, Herman?'

'No,' he answers, curt to incivility; 'I remember nothing. I drowned my memory ever so many years ago in the waters of Lethe. I know that there is a hamlet called Tipsbury on the ordnance-map, but I know no more.'

'What a nice thing that Lethe must be!' retorts Myra, coiling up, as the Americans say. 'I wish they would import the water, like Apollinaris. Many people I know seem to wash out their memories with soda-and-brandy. I fancy that is the modern Lethe. Now let us be business-like, and talk of our comedy.'

It is something to be able to say 'our,' even of this child of his brain; something that she can give form and life to the creations of his fancy; something to help him by a suggestion, to direct him by her taste, which is faultless in all the details of dramatic art, from the turn of an epigram to the length of a ballet-dancer's petticoat. They talk drama for the next half hour vigorously, and Myra helps her author by more than one subtle suggestion, shows him where his scaffolding is weak, and how the climax of an act may be intensified. In his gratitude he admires her almost as much as that innocent Myra of years gone by who acted the sleeping scene in *Macbeth* in the children's parlour at Colehaven Vicarage.

The race for the Cup comes on at last, after a good many races, which seem slightly uninteresting to the masses, though the cause of maddest bawling and convulsive throes, as of Dionysian possession, to the bookmen. Now every one is, or pretends to be, interested; every glass follows the favourite in the preliminary canter, which some eager spirits mistake for the race itself. Miss Belormond has backed the favourite, and is to win gloves. Mrs. Brandreth has haughtily refused to speculate in any manner.

Very far away from that crowded racecourse are Myra's thoughts, even while the horses are sweeping past, as if driven before the blast of a hurricane, and the voices below are clamouring loudest. She is thinking of Colehaven and the days that are gone— the careless days, brimful of happiness, when Herman was hers. Perhaps it is that sweet time of youth she regrets almost as much as her lost lover; perhaps she exaggerates that vanished happiness, and takes it for something better than it was, being so utterly gone. However this may be, regret is bitter. She sits beside her sometime lover, and knows herself as far from him as if they had the Southern Sea between them. And yet to-day her mind is fluttered with faint hopes. He has seemed happy, amused, interested. Her power to charm him may not be quite lost even yet.

They leave the course immediately after the great race, Myra and Miss Belormond being due on the stage at half-past eight; and a twenty-eight mile drive being no trifle, even with fresh horses at Hounslow. Throughout that homeward drive Mrs. Brandreth is bright and animated as when they journeyed by the same road in the morning. She has put the past and future out of her mind, and thinks only of being agreeable in the present. She has an instinctive consciousness that sentiment will avail her nothing with Herman. His assailable side is worldly: æsthetic, artistic perhaps, but assuredly not romantic. She lays about her at her will with that reckless wit of hers—a mere effervescence of the moment, and hardly worth remembrance, but sharp enough to be refreshing to jaded spirits. Lord Earlswood, who has exchanged places with Lyndhurst for the return, is in raptures.

'I can't think where you get your ideas,' he exclaims; 'they are so far-fetched, yet they seem to come to you so naturally.'

'They grow wild, like other weeds,' replies Myra. 'I keep no intellectual forcing pit.'

'Most people's clever hits are grown under glass,' says Earlswood, quick to take up anybody else's notion. 'Their sharpness is like the acidity of untimely peaches.'

Miss Belormond thinks her companions might as well talk French at once—it would hardly be ruder to employ that unknown tongue than to discourse in a jargon like this, which, for all she knows, may veil some sarcastic allusions to herself. This young lady, who has graduated at a Peckham day-school, is apt to be afflicted with an uneasy suspicion of educated people. She, indeed, half believes that education is another name for refined malice.

It is only seven o'clock when they reach Hyde Park-corner.

'Come to my rooms and have tea,' says Herman, who has a feeling that this holiday of his cannot last too long.

'O, how nice that would be!' exclaims Miss Belormond, who has brightened a little under the influence of a few civil speeches from Lord Earlswood. 'I never feel fit for anything if I go without my cup of tea.'

'You shall have your cup of tea, Miss Belormond. You'll stop, won't you, Myra? You can spare half an hour.'

Rarely of late has he called her Myra. The shining hazel eyes look at him dreamily for a moment or so before she answers.

'Half an hour, and ten minutes more to drive to the theatre; that will leave us nearly an hour to dress. Yes, I think we could manage it; couldn't we, Belormond?'

Belormond is sure it can be managed. She has a wonderful idea of Mr. Westray—a vague notion that an author is a compendium of everybody else's cleverness, and that this particular author is always inwardly laughing at her. She is grateful for any civility from him, and is curious to know what kind of place an author lives in. She had supposed the abode of the species to be mostly in garrets, when not in the Queen's Bench, and has been not a little surprised at discovering that Herman inhabits Piccadilly.

Myra, too, has a gentle curiosity about Herman's lodgings. How well she remembers his room at the Vicarage!—room which she has coyly peeped into over her sister's shoulder when the proprietor of the chamber was out of the way. Such a narrow den! a mere slip off another room, meant for a dressing closet, but used as a study! A shelf or two of shabby books—the father's college books handed down to the son—a battered old desk by the open window, a bunch of honeysuckle and roses in a brown jar on the window-sill, pipes, gun, fishing-rod, foils, and single-sticks in a conglomerated heap in the corner, and a collection of Tenniel's cartoons wafered against the faded paper.

The landau pulls up before the door of a tall house facing the Green Park, and Herman hands the ladies to the pavement. His latch-key opens the door, and they go up a great many stairs.

'He does live in a garret, after all,' thinks Belormond, pleased with her own sagacity.

Herman stops on the second-floor landing, however, and opens the door of a large airy room, with a bay window and a wide substantial balcony—such a balcony to smoke and muse in upon warm summer nights, with a glimpse of minster and senate-house yonder across the tree-tops to inspire the ambitious dreamer.

It is a large room, simply furnished; not lined with books from floor to ceiling, for Westray is too much a man of the world to be a book collector. There is a bookcase on either side of the fireplace— one containing books of reference only, the other just those choicest of the world's classics, to know which is to have skimmed the cream of the human intellect.

The writing-table occupies the centre of the room, and is large enough for a solicitor in full practice. A capacious sofa, half a dozen delightful arm-chairs, various in shape, age, and material, a Sutherland table, and a handy-looking sideboard and cellaret, complete the furniture of this apartment, which is study and living-room in one. Some fine photographs of Gérôme's pictures adorn the walls.

'Quite a bachelor's tent,' says Myra. 'Looks as if it could be lifted easily.'

Herman orders tea instantly.

'I daresay the kettle's off the boil,' says Miss Belormond. 'It's so difficult to get boiling water in lodgings; at least I find it so, though I pay three guineas a week and extras. They're quite put out if I want a cup of tea promiscuously.'

'You should get them into better training, Miss Belormond,' retorts Herman. 'I am always demanding promiscuous cups of tea, and the slavey is as brisk as Aladdin's genius.'

The slavey, a sedate-looking housemaid of thirty odd, justifies his praise by appearing promptly with tea-tray and urn, and all appliances to boot—London cream, strawberries, pound-cake, wafer biscuits from the adjacent confectioner's. The Sutherland table is drawn into the bay, and they sit down to tea, Myra in the post of honour. Herman remembers that afternoon tea at Lochwithian with a rather guilty feeling; yet there can be very little harm, if any, in showing this small civility to an old friend.

The half hour goes very quickly, and then Herman puts the ladies back into the carriage, shakes hands with both, and strolls off with Lyndhurst to dine at the Agora.

'Wonderfully fascinating woman, Mrs. Brandreth,' says Lyndhurst. 'You're a lucky fellow, Westray.'

'Lucky because Mrs. Brandreth is fascinating? that's a *non sequiter*.'

'But you don't mean to say that—that there isn't some understanding—that you are not going to marry her?' blurts out Lyndhurst, with his charming candour. 'Somebody told me quite a romantic story: that you were engaged years ago, before she married Brandreth, and that when you met afterwards, you both discovered that you had never ceased to care for each other, and so on—the sort of thing they put into novels.'

'It is the misfortune of such a position as Mrs. Brandreth's that the world is inventive, and that when a lady's life happens to be particularly uneventful, people's imaginations supply the void with plausible fiction. Mrs. Brandreth to me is simply Mrs. Brandreth; a very charming woman, whose talents I admire, whose force of character I respect.'

'But you're not engaged to her? Well, that's curious; I thought it was an established fact. Certainly Earlswood has contrived to get her a good deal talked about; but we, who are in a manner behind the scenes, know there's nothing in that.'

'I consider Mrs. Brandreth a woman of perfectly undamaged reputation,' replies Herman, 'if that's what you mean. It merely happens that she and I are friends, and not lovers. If I had any warmer feeling for her than friendship, there is nothing in her past or her present life that would urge me to stifle it.'

'That's very generously expressed,' says Lyndhurst. 'You fellows who write books have such a knack of turning a sentence. O, by the way, who was that charming young lady I met you with at the Frivolity a month or two ago—a tall girl, dignified, indeed rather haughty-looking, but with a sort of rustic freshness about her?'

'That young lady is Miss Morcombe, the daughter of a Welsh gentleman.'

'Welsh! Dear me; I thought they wore conical hats and short petticoats.'

'I believe some of the peasantry do indulge in those eccentricities, but not in the neighbourhood of Mr. Morcombe's estate.'

'So,' thought Lyndhurst, 'Mr. Morecombe is a landed gentleman, and that lovely girl has money. Artful card this Westray.'

They dine together generously, and Herman, going back to his chambers late at night, feels that he has wasted his day, or, in his own stronger language, 'given a day to Belial.'

CHAPTER II.

> 'She is mine own ;
> And I as rich in having such a Jewel,
> As twenty seas, if all their sand were pearl,
> The water nectar, and the rocks pure gold.'

HERMAN goes house-hunting soon after that Ascot Cup-day, goes in search of the nest that is to shelter his tender dove by and by. He explores Chiswick —dear little humble unpretentious Chiswick, which is old still while all the rest of the world is new— but Chiswick being limited in its capacities, and having its nicest nooks and corners filled, does not offer him just that dainty little water-side villa he desires to find; so he harks back to Fulham, and there, not far from Putney bridge, discovers a modest dwelling, with a narrow lawn sloping to the Thames; a house once occupied by a famous wit, and which seems to him the better for the association, though the wit's life was but a marred and broken existence at best.

The house is not especially convenient or well built, but the drawing-room and two rooms over, which will do for bedroom and boudoir, Herman thinks, are pretty. There are windows opening on the lawn, a verandah, a balcony above—all those adjuncts which a man looks for, when he ought to be examining the kitchen range and inquiring if there is a copper. Herman is pleased, and, lest the chance should slip through his fingers, takes the house on a repairing lease without delay, his tenancy to begin from the midsummer quarter.

This important step taken, he engages an ancient female of the charwoman species to take charge of the house, and goes forthwith to Messrs. Molding and Korness, an expensive and fashionable firm of decorators and upholsterers, and gives them carte-blanche to make his house perfect after its kind.

'I don't want expensive decoration or furniture,' he says, thinking himself passing prudent the while. 'Let everything be of the simplest, but in exquisite taste. As taste is your business I shall not interfere unnecessarily. Let the prevailing tone of the drawing-room be white and pale seagreen,' he adds, remembering Ruth's room at Lochwithian.

The upholsterer's man bows and smiles, and ventures to hope he shall give satisfaction.

'Perhaps you would like to look round, sir, with a view to making your own selection,' says the man; 'all our goods are marked in plain figures:' as if that made them cheaper.

Herman acquiesces, and perambulates a thicket of chairs, and then a forest fo Arabian beds, and then a city of dining-tables, and a necropolis of wardrobes, all like family tombs.

'Dear me, how uninteresting furniture looks when it comes to be classified!' he exclaims. 'I don't feel capable of choosing anything. I think I'll send you a rough drawing of the style of room I like, and you can carry it out in your own way.'

The upholsterer is charmed with the suggestion. He sees his way to something rather expensive in the way of joinery.

To a lady's cabriole lounging chair, in ebonised wood, made after your own design . . £16 16 0
To a gentleman's Etruscan do. do., cabriole legs, also made to own design 17 17 0

This is the kind of entry which presents itself to the upholsterer's mental vision as he bows his customer out. Herman thinks of his loose thousands, and resolves that his darling's nest shall be as bright as taste and money can make it. She shall not be made to feel that she has wasted herself on a pauper, or that she has lost too much in refusing Vivian Hetheridge's wealth and status.

He writes to tell her that 'our house' is taken, and that he will come to Lochwithian next week if he may. He turns his back upon London one fair July morning, gladly as a boy let loose from school. He has sent Myra Brandreth the first two acts of a comedy, but has not seen her since the Cup-day, and he reserves the final act and the conclusion of his novel as work to be done in the tranquil atmosphere of Lochwithian. He will have his working hours there, he thinks; an hour or two between breakfast and luncheon sometimes, an hour or two stolen from the night.

How sweet the hills and valleys seem to him, when Shrewsbury is left behind, and the placid fertility of Midland landscape gives place to romantic

Wales—wooded hills, winding streams, dry some of them in this peerless summer time, one but a bare bed of bleached pebbles gleaming whitely athwart brushwood and saplings! He remembers the last time he travelled by this single line, piercing its iron way through the cloven heart of the hills, and always ascending at a very palpable elevation, till the air blows fresher and keener, and he seems to enter a purer world. He was going back to London smoke and London worldliness on that occasion, going downwards, and Editha Morcombe was no more to him than a lovely and noble-minded woman, utterly remote from his life.

Just in the sultriest hour of the sultry day the train, reduced to half a dozen carriages of Tenbyites, slackens its pace, and comes slowly past the sprinkling of labouring men's cottages and smart modern villas which forms the outskirts of Llandrysak. There is the little station—refreshment-room, bookstall, all *en règle;* the two brisk porters, ready to carry your luggage to the loftiest eeric among the surrounding hills; the placid station-master, who looks as if he had never heard of a railway accident; and last, not least, the entire population of Llandrysak turned out to witness the arrival of the train. There they sit in an awe-inspiring row, as many at least as the benches will accommodate, the rest standing, and all glaring at the new-comers.

Herman regards these aborigines no more than if they had been so many rows of cabbages in the station-master's garden, for yonder above the boundary of the station he sees a sociable and pair, with a clerical gentleman sitting in front with the coachman, and a lady seated behind; a lady who smiles at him from under the shade of an Indian silk umbrella, a lady to whom his heart goes forth with a glad bound.

The clerical gentleman, scrambling down as the train stops, reveals the features of Mr. Petherick, the incumbent of Lochwithian, and is on the platform by the time Herman has alighted, ready to help in looking after the luggage. A large portmanteau, dressing-bag, and despatch-box are speedily selected from the varieties of property disgorged by the van, and hoisted into the front of the sociable, filling the space lately occupied by Mr. Petherick. Herman leaves that amiable parson the entire responsibility of the luggage, while he hurries to Editha and clasps the dear hand, almost too deeply moved for speech. Forgotten in that moment every thought or hope that is not of her or for her. How lovely the scene appears to him—the circle of hills, the warmth and glow of the summer afternoon, the distant farmhouses here and there, white against the green, the utter peacefulness of all things round him! The quiet of the landscape steals into his breast like balm, and as he takes his place beside Editha he has that reposeful bliss which comes to us sometimes in a happy dream—some vision in which the dead return and the days of our youth are renewed.

'Perhaps it would be better to put the portmanteau behind, Editha, if you don't mind it,' says the brisk voice of Mr. Petherick, who feels that he may be rather in the way should he intrude his earthly presence upon these two dreamers. Editha looks up at him with a gentle smile of unconsciousness, not in the least aware what he means, just at this particular moment having lost the understanding of her mother tongue save when spoken by Herman. So Mr. Petherick shunts the portmanteau from the box to the body of the sociable, and resumes his seat by the coachman, leaving Herman and Editha alone in their paradise.

'How good of you to meet me!' exclaims Herman.

'How good of you to come ever so much earlier than you promised!' responds Editha; after which original remarks they lapse into fatuous silence for some moments, contemplating each other's faces as the sociable rolls past the outskirts of Llandrysak, and crosses a wide expanse of common where the furze bushes outshine the Field of Cloth-of-gold, and tiny pools of water gleam like jewels in the sun. The lark sings high above them, carolling as for very gladness at their reunion.

'How pleased nature seems to see us together again!' says Herman, with a happy laugh. 'There seems a note wanting in the harmony of the universe when we two are parted.'

'Do you really mean that you have been so

foolish as to take a house, Herman, or was that part of your letter a joke?'

'A joke for which I am to pay a hundred and twenty pounds a year, love, to say nothing of taxes—a joke which Molding and Korness of Oxford-street are going to furnish. It will be ready by our wedding-day in September, so if we get tired of Switzerland sooner than we suppose we shall, our home will be swept and garnished for our reception.'

'Our home! how strange that sounds, Herman!'

'Sweeter than strange, dear.'

'But you talk of our wedding as if it were settled for September.'

'Isn't it? I thought we came to that understanding.'

'No, indeed; I was to have at least a year at home with Ruth—time enough for her to accustom herself to the idea of our separation.'

'There is to be no such thing as separation. You and I will often run down to Lochwithian for a week or two, if your father will allow us.'

'As if papa would not be glad to have us!'

'And your sister can come to us at least twice a year. Travelling is made easy nowadays, even for an invalid.'

'Ruth has been so good!' exclaims Editha.

In this first half hour of reunion they are both inclined to be discursive, not finishing up one subject thoroughly, but starting off at a tangent every now and then.

'How good, dearest?'

'Why, dear, just at first the thought of our engagement made her rather unhappy. She is so much attached to Mr. Hetheridge, and you, of course, are a comparative stranger. She asked me so many questions about you, Herman—your principles, your ideas upon serious subjects—questions I hardly knew how to answer. We seem so seldom to have talked seriously.'

'My love, we are not a convocation of Churchmen, or a Quakers' meeting, or an assembly of Scottish Presbyterians. What would you have us talk about but ourselves and our own happiness?'

'But I told her how good you are, Herman—how full of noble ambition and refined feelings; and then that last book of yours—that quite won her heart. So, little by little, she grew reconciled to the idea of our marriage.'

'What ineffable goodness!' cries Herman, somewhat piqued. It is not pleasant to be received with stinted welcome, even into the best of families.

'O Herman, how unkindly you say that! You must not speak of Ruth with a sneer if you love me.'

'If I love you, little one!' he echoes tenderly, drawing her nearer to him (that good parson Petherick is placidly contemplative of the landscape). 'If I love you! There are no ifs in such love as mine. But it's hardly a pleasant thing to learn that one is to be received as the serpent that crept into Eden. Is it Hetheridge's old family or large estate which has won your sister's heart?'

'Neither, dear. She likes him because he is so good and true.'

'And she harbours a lurking notion that I must needs be bad and false—an incarnation of city vices as opposed to rustic virtues. I think you would have grown weary of Mr. Hetheridge's provincial perfection, my pet, in the lasting *tête-à-tête* of matrimony.'

'Let us talk about the house, Herman. How pretty it must be!'

Hereupon follows a vivid description of the Fulham villa: the river—the clumsy old wooden bridge —Putney church, grave and gray—the episcopal palace with its shady garden—the secluded quiet of the place.

'I have had such a happy idea about the dining-room,' says Herman. 'You remember the scene in *Hemlock*, the Pompeian triclinium?'

'Perfectly.'

'Well, I have told Molding and Korness to make our hall and dining-room Pompeian. The success of *Hemlock* will very well balance any extravagance in the suggestion.'

'What a charming idea!' exclaims Editha; 'but isn't it wrong to spend so much money upon furnishing, Herman? We are not going to be rich.'

'My love, do you remember what Dr. Johnson said about Thrale's brewery, when the business was being sold? "We are not here to sell a parcel of boilers and vats, but the potentiality of growing rich beyond the dreams of avarice." Do you hold literature as something less than beer, and are you going to limit my power of increasing our income? You do not know what strength I shall have to labour, dear, when I have given hostages to Fortune.'

'Dear Herman, how brave you are!' she cries admiringly, as if he stood on the topmost rung of a scaling-ladder in a storm of shot and shell; 'but the humblest home you could make for me would be just as dear as the finest house your successful work can win. I want to be your helpmate, not a burden to you.'

They are driving up to the porch at Lochwithian by this time. The old dogs lie basking in the sunshine; the old-fashioned flower-beds are full of bloom. The fishpond and the fountain, the crumbling old red walls where the peaches and apricots are ripening, smile at him as in welcome. Every familiar feature of the place is the same as when he saw it first just a year ago; the only difference is that the Editha of last year was a stately stranger about whom he thought with vague wonder, while the Editha of today is his very own—his wife that is to be.

'Darling,' he whispers with a little gush of emotion, 'I am so happy when I think of last year and this.'

'Come to see Ruth,' says Editha directly they have alighted. She leads him straightway up the shallow old oaken staircase, past the newel over which he remembers her looking down at him when they parted, along the shadowy corridor where stand old blue-delf jars crammed with rose-leaves, and into the white panelled parlour where the invalid sister reclines, just as he saw her first, in spotless cambric morning robe, with a knot of coloured ribbon here and there among the soft white drapery.

'He has come, Ruth,' cries Editha, as if this arrival, formally announced by letter two days ago, were something wonderful.

'I am very glad,' replies Ruth softly, in that gentle voice of hers which has a touch of pathos at times. 'How do you do, Herman? Welcome to Lochwithian, brother. We are brother and sister henceforward, are we not? bound to each other by our common love for Editha.'

'I hope to be not all unworthy to claim a brother's name,' says Herman, kissing the hand that lies trustingly in his. He feels that, in his character of serpent, he has been received with no small indulgence. 'I fear you must hate me for coming here to steal your darling,' he says humbly.

Ruth's grave eyes seem to be looking him through and through, perusing all the flaws and specks and knots in the grain of his nature.

'I am not quite selfish enough for that,' she answers sadly, 'though it has been one of my prayers that Editha's home and mine should never lie far apart. But my chief thought and desire must always be for her happiness. If it is happier for her that we should live apart, so be it. I am content.'

Editha and Ruth have clasped hands, the younger girl kneeling by her sister's couch.

'We are never to be long apart, dearest,' says Editha. 'I am coming home to see you and papa at least three times a year, and you are coming to us twice in the year; that will leave short intervals of separation.'

'Our home will be yours, Ruth,' says Herman. 'It shall not be our fault if it is not made pleasant to you.'

'I will come to you some day, if God gives me strength,' answers Ruth, her eyes clouded with tears, but a smile on the sensitive mouth. 'It will be sweet to me to see my pet in her new home—to see her happy and beloved.'

After this all doleful thoughts are dismissed. They talk of the house at Fulham—the Pompeian hall and dining-room; the drawing-room, which is to be furnished like a room in a Dutch picture, after a drawing of Herman's; garden small, but sheltered by a few good old trees, and altogether perfect in its way.

'A garden where we can take our coffee on summer evenings, Editha,' adds Herman, 'and where I can lie at your feet thinking out my work, while you watch the boats gliding past, silent as shadows, on the starlit river.'

How sweet it all sounds, and to Ruth's ear how

vague! Editha gazes up at her lover with ineffable rapture—her poet lover; for to her mind he is no less than a poet—a creature apart, gifted with an unsurpassable birthright. She believes that every feeling of his, every fancy, every desire is of a finer texture than the feelings, fancies, and desires of ordinary mankind. The bitter truth that in common things your poet is apt to be no better than common men has yet to be revealed to her.

Ruth thinks of honest, earnest, single-minded Vivian, and wonders whether a man who lives by the cultivation of his fancy, and must in some measure be the slave of his fancy, whose temper is irritated by a perpetual struggle to excel, will ever make as good a husband as that simple-hearted Radnorshire squire. Will the time ever come when either of these two—all in all to each other to-day, and seeing nothing in life beyond—will find a something wanting in their union, a sense of something missed, something that might have been, and is not? That 'might have been' is the curse of your poetic temperament. The lovers leave Ruth and wander out into the garden by and by, and through the great stable-yard, and across an ancient orchard to the ruins, and Herman renews his acquaintance with scenes and objects in which he has henceforward a personal interest. They stroll together by the narrow river, where the forget-me-nots are blooming just as they bloomed last year; and they look up at the solemn hills which have outlasted Lochwithian Priory, and taste that utter and perfect happiness which only such lovers know—lovers whose future lies before them smooth as some placid lake shining under the summer sun.

The Squire receives his future son-in-law heartily, not because he is reconciled to the match—which he is not—but because he is too hospitable a man to be otherwise than cordial to his guest. One of the prettiest rooms in the Priory has been allotted to Herman—a room at one end of the rambling old house, with an oriel window overlooking the shrubbery and the church in the hollow beneath.

'I shall hear the bell ringing for early service of a morning, and be reminded that there are God-fearing men and women in this out-of-the-way corner of the land. I wish I could follow their footsteps, and feel that I was doing good for my soul,' Herman says to himself with a sigh, as he looks out of his window before dressing for dinner.

Time glides by with a divine quiet at Lochwithian. There is a dinner at the Priory soon after his arrival, and Herman is presented to the county families resident within visiting distance. Other dinners follow to which Herman is bidden, and he feels that he is received and accepted as Editha's future husband; but the dinner parties hardly make any break in these halcyon days of his life. They are very quiet gatherings, and he is generally allowed to have Editha all to himself for the greater part of the time, so that the dinner parties in a manner resolve themselves into delicious assemblies of two. Editha and he are seated apart at an open window; or they stroll out into the moonlit garden to look at the roses; or they linger in a conservatory because the rooms are warm. Everybody is indulgent to them, and they are petted and humoured as if they were children.

'Rather humiliating, isn't it, darling, that our

condition should be so obvious to every one?' says Herman; whereupon Editha laughs and blushes, and rearranges the spray of maiden-hair which she pinned in his coat in the hall at Lochwithian. She feels even in this small matter of providing a flower for his button-hole that she is beginning her duties as a wife.

They are about together all through the happy summer days; sometimes no farther than the garden or the ruins—sometimes riding with the Squire—sometimes climbing the hills or exploring distant villages with Mr. Petherick and his trusty dogs for their companions. One day they spend the sultry afternoon quite alone on the bank of the Pennant, which at one romantic spot rushes like a cataract between steep walls of moss-greened crag—rocky boulders in whose cleft and crevices tender ferns grow thick and green. There is a narrow and somewhat perilous wooden bridge across this torrent, which is one of the features of the neighbourhood.

Here Editha and Herman have seated themselves in the sultry after-luncheon hours, sheltered by a tangled mass of greenery, in which oak, ash, and alder, birch and sycamore, are mixed together anyhow, for beneath the crags there is abundance of dark rick loam in which the gnarled roots find their sustenance.

Editha is seated on a low bank, hemming a child's pinafore—those busy fingers of hers clothe half the cottage children about Lochwithian. Herman lies at her feet, looking up at little flecks of warm blue sky shining among the tangled leaves. The sun steeps that summer roof and sheds a greenish light, as through the stained glass of a minster window.

Herman yawns and then sighs—the yawn expresses the blissfulness of repose, the sigh is in self-reproach.

'Not a line written since I came to Lochwithian,' he says, 'and I meant to be so industrious.'

'I try to leave your mornings free always, Herman; but you come strolling out into the garden or down to the village just when I fancy you are so busy.'

'Elective affinity, dearest. I find myself drawn

towards you whether I will or not. I open my desk, and dip my pen in the ink, and wait for an idea. But when the idea comes it is only Editha. What is Editha doing? I must go and look for Editha. That is the nearest approach to an idea that I can dig out of my inner consciousness. The fact is, I am too happy to be industrious. If you do not consent to our being married very soon, Editha, I shall be a ruined man.'

'You expect to be not quite so happy when we are married,' says Editha, smiling at the little pinafore.

'No, love, but to be less tumultuously blest. There will be a placid certainty—the knowledge that you are mine till the end of my days, the sense that our life is laid down in a groove, and that we have nothing to do but travel smoothly on. When we come back from Switzerland, and I settle down in my own little den at Fulham—my books of reference at my elbow, my publisher getting impatient—I shall write as if by steam. Here every bird's song is an invocation to the spirit of idleness. Shall it be the fifteenth of September, love?' he pleads, raising himself upon his elbow, and bringing himself nearer Editha, so near that he is in some danger of having his countenance wounded by that busy needle.

He is talking of his wedding-day, which has been a subject of discussion between them for some time.

'Dear Herman, you know that I want one more year at home,' replies Editha seriously; 'I want to spend another year with Ruth, and among the poor people I have known so long. I want to wind up my life here deliberately, and not snap the thread suddenly as if I had grown tired of home and those who love me.'

'Another year! My dear Editha, be reasonable. Think of the house taken and furnished, rent running on, taxes, furniture spoiling, walls mildewing, gilding tarnishing.'

'It was foolish of you to take a house so hurriedly,' says Editha reproachfully.

'Foolish to build my nest after St. Valentine's-day? Editha, am I to think that a few old women, affecting piety with an eye to the loaves and fishes —a flock of drawling nasal school-children, who know more of the multiplication table than their limited finances will ever bring into play—are to come between you and me, and doom me to a year of unsettled and solitary existence?'

'I am thinking of Ruth as well as of my pensioners and school-children.'

'Put Ruth out of the question. We have settled that Ruth is to lose very little of your society after you are married. I wish you'd put down that pinafore, Editha; the click-click of the needle disturbs the serenity of the atmosphere.'

Editha obeys without a word. She is likely to be that traitor in the camp of strong-minded womanhood, an obedient wife. Herman takes the industrious hand prisoner, and holds it during the rest of his discourse.

'Dear love, why should we not be married soon? My life is broken, disorganised, out of joint, till we begin the world together in our new home.'

A little more persuasion, and she yields the point. Ruth has told her that, if she is sure of her lover's worthiness, there is nothing to be gained by a long engagement. Her father is indifferent, seeing that she is determined to marry Herman Westray, whether the marriage be soon or late. Of herself, unaided, she is not strong enough to oppose Herman's wish; so it is settled that the marriage is to take place on the fifteenth of September, which, the almanac informs them, falls on a Thursday. They are at the end of July already, but the question of her trousseau not being paramount with Editha, it does not occur to her to protest that six weeks are much too short for preparation, from a dressmaker's point of view. She has no idea of spending half her small capital in finery. Her plentifully furnished wardrobe, her stock of rare old lace, inherited from her mother, will need no large additions to be ample for the requirements of a young matron. Very far from her thoughts are wedding finery and wedding festivities. She is inclined to search deeper into the beginning of things.

'Herman, what first made you think of me?' she asks, looking at his upturned face as he leans on his elbow, his head thrown back a little, his eyes lifted to hers. 'Our lives lie so far apart.'

'Perhaps that was the very fact that set me thinking of you,' he answers, quite willing to be questioned, rather pleased indeed to analyse his feelings. 'You came into my life like a creature out of a purer and better world, and my heart went to you naturally. If I had met you at a ball, just in the beaten way of society, I might have thought you the handsomest woman in the room, but I should hardly have known you to be the one woman among all womankind whose love were best worth winning.'

'I don't quite understand how you were to find that out here,' Editha replies, smiling at his praise. 'First, I am a very ordinary person; and next, you saw very little of me.'

'I heard your praises from others, and I saw you in your home, with your sister—the giver of gladness in your narrow circle. I saw and heard enough to send me away with your image in my heart. I did not surrender myself too readily; I made believe to myself that I was not in love with you; but the book I wrote last winter was one long tête-à-tête with you, and I was perfectly wretched till we met again.'

'Herman,' Editha says gravely, coming to that one awful question which no woman can refrain from asking—though the answer, if honestly given, is sure to make her miserable—' did you ever care for any one else? Your first love—to whom was that given, and why did it end unhappily?'

Herman winces slightly at the question.

' First love, Editha, is the offspring of fancy, and has its source in the brain rather than the heart. First love is like one's first champagne—a transient intoxication. Mine came to a very prosaic end. The lady jilted me, dismissed me without a day's warning.'

' Then she must have been unworthy of you.'

'Not unworthy of me, perhaps, but unworthy of my regret. I was wise enough to discover that in time, and wasted none upon her,' adds Herman carelessly.

Editha is grateful for his candour, and yet a little disappointed, for it would have been so much sweeter if Herman could have told her that she herself was his first love.

'Were you very much in love with the lady?'

she asks, taking up the little pinafore again, and smoothing down the hem with extreme nicety.

'Over head and ears; but it was calf-love remember. The girl was accomplished, diabolically clever; not absolutely beautiful, but graceful beyond measure. Just the kind of girl to bewitch an undergraduate. I thought her simply the most charming creature I had ever seen or dreamed of. We had been children together, and one day she beamed upon me suddenly as a woman.'

'You had known each other from childhood! Then she must have loved you. Perhaps she was influenced by others when she jilted you,' hazards Editha, slow to believe that any one could voluntarily play him false.

'Possibly.'

'Did she marry for money?'

'The man she married had expectations, I believe, but they were never realised. He died a few years after his marriage, and left his widow in very indifferent circumstances.'

'Have you ever seen her since then?'

This is trying. Herman digs his elbow into

a little hillock of moss, and endeavours to look unconcerned.

'Yes, I have met her, once in a way, in society.'

'But not often?'

'No; our lives lie far apart. Editha,' he adds solemnly, seeing the cloud upon her face, 'be jealous neither of the past nor of the future. No rival can ever come between us two.'

'Are you quite sure of that, Herman?'

'As sure as that I live and hold your hand in mine,' he answers, clasping it fondly.

'Because, if there is the shadow of doubt in your mind, leave me my old life. When we are married, and I have left home and father and sister, and everybody and everything I have loved and lived for until now, for your sake, I shall be unreasonably exacting perhaps, and ask for more than you can give, if you cannot give me all your heart.'

'It is yours, love—yours and no other's. It went forth to you gladly, as a bird flies to meet the summer. It is yours for ever and ever—the for ever of man's brief span.'

'Mine in God's for ever, I trust,' she answers

solemnly. 'I cannot imagine a heaven in which we shall not see and know our friends again.'

Herman kisses the fair white hand for sole reply: and they are happy; fondly believing in each other and a love unassailable by time or change.

CHAPTER III.

'So, she leaning on her husband's arm, they turned homeward by a rosy path which the gracious sun struck out for them in its setting. And O there are days in this life worth life and worth death. And O what a bright old song it is, that O 'tis love, 'tis love, 'tis love, that makes the world go round.'

It is the last week, the last day of Editha's home life. All that she has loved and tended and created and cared for in that placid circle of home is to be surrendered at eleven o'clock to-morrow morning in favour of Herman Westray. She may come back to Lochwithian Priory—she means to return thither often—but it will be as a guest and in some measure a stranger. She is touched with sadness on this bright September morning as she counts her loss, wandering slowly round the old gardens alone, saying good-bye to every rose-tree and all the familiar flowers in the humble little greenhouses that have been paid for with her pocket-money and built after her own design. To all intents and purposes she has been sole mistress of Lochwithian Priory for the last five years, Ruth being no more than adviser, and the Squire content to rub along easily, just able to meet the demands of his bailiff, who hungers for machinery on the home-farm, and is eager to follow the march of agricultural progress.

Here, by the fountain on whose margin they sat when first he came to the Priory, Herman finds his betrothed. She is looking at the restless goldfish dreamily, with a cluster of tea-roses in her hand.

'Dear love, I have been looking for you everywhere. What, the waterworks turned on already, Editha? I thought young ladies reserved the supply for the wedding morning.'

'I have been saying good-bye to the garden, Herman,' she answers, smiling through her tears.

'You should have made it *au revoir*, dearest.'

'It will never be my garden any more, Herman.'

'And for sole exchange I give you a lawn about the size of a tablecloth, with one immemorial elm, a weeping-willow, a tree or two of the coniferous tribe, an ancient mulberry in the corner, and a pink horse-chestnut. A remarkable collection, I think, for a suburban garden.'

'I feel sure that it is lovely,' she answers, looking across the valley to the steep green slopes beyond, with one bold hill that seems to touch the sky. 'It will be so nice to have the river flowing past our lawn; but I am afraid that just at first I shall miss the hills. They are a part of my life, somehow. One of the first things I can remember is standing on the top of that green peak looking down at the Priory, all the windows shining in the evening sun, and thinking that the house was lighted for a grand party. I was quite a little child, and had strayed out of the garden and climbed the hill by myself, and was half way down again before my nurse found me.'

'Enterprising little soul! We will take a holiday in the hill country twice a year, Editha. You shall not suffer nostalgia. And, remember, I am going to introduce you to the monarch of mountains, so you needn't weep for these Cambrian ant-hills. What are you going to do with yourself all day?'

Herman has only returned from London the day before yesterday, and is residing on this occasion under Mr. Petherick's hospitable roof, but contrives nevertheless to spend most of his time with Editha.

'I must say good-bye to the people at Llanmoel.'

'Is that the eccentric little settlement at the base of that great hill you showed me the other day?'

'Yes.'

'Let us set off at once, then, and make a day of it.'

'But I am afraid it will tire you, Herman. It is a long walk, and there are several people I want to see. And then Mr. Petherick may think it unkind of you to desert him.'

'That best of men has given me my liberty till we meet at your father's dinner-table. And as to being tired of a long day with you, love—why, it will be an instalment of our honeymoon.'

They set out together in the fresh bright noontide, Herman carrying a good-sized basket full of keepsakes for Editha's pensioners—young women she has taught as children when no more than a child herself; old people she has ministered to almost from her babyhood, when she went with her nurse to carry small comforts to the poorest among the peasantry, fair as a child-angel to their delighted eyes.

Their way lies for the most part through meadows —meadows of all shapes and sizes—with high tangled hedgerows and steep ferny banks, which remind Herman of his native Devonshire, and just a little of that summer day when Myra Clitheroe promised to forego fame for his sake. From the last of the meadows they emerge on the bank of the Pennant, cross a rustic suspension bridge, and enter a hilly road, little more than a lane as to width, and as stony as it is picturesque.

They talk for a long time of Herman's books, past, present, and to come, in which Editha is intensely interested. She will not be one of those wives who prefer the *Family Herald* to their husband's masterpieces, or who look upon a new novel from the marital pen as the source of a new drawing-room carpet. She questions him closely about the shadows of his brain, and he finds that his creations are more real to her than they are even to himself.

'You must have been deeply in love that first time, Herman, or you could never have written your first novel,' she says, that first romance being a record of passionate disappointed love.

'My dearest, I am happy to say I never committed forgery, yet the critics were good enough to pronounce that the fraudulent banker's clerk in my second novel is very true to life.'

Editha shakes her head dubiously. She is not able to explain her convictions, but she feels that the mechanism of that second novel is art, while the passion of love and anger in the first is nature.

He tells her the plan of his new book—the story which is half written, and which he stands pledged to complete before Christmas—and finds it very pleasant to confide his ideas to a thoroughly sympathetic companion. He is not a man prone to impart his fancies, but he finds a new habit growing upon him since he and Editha have been plighted lovers. He is not content nowadays till he has told her his last inspiration.

They loiter on the way a good deal, and it is two o'clock when they ascend the stony lane. There is another meadow to cross before they come to Llanmoel, which secluded village is not on any particular road, but seems to have been dropped down anyhow among the fields. A meadow brings them to the church, which in architectural pretensions might be a barn, and which modestly hides itself under an enormous yew—a yew so gigantic and intrusive that one great branch has grown close up to the church wall, and has had to be lopped lest it should knock down that rural temple.

Grazing placidly among the lopsided tombstones, Herman and Editha find a donkey, evidently belonging to some privileged freeholder, and serenely indifferent to their approach. The clumsy old porch of plaster and woodwork, ivy-grown, with a Norman arch over the church-door, and a little bit of quaintly carven stonework, whereon blunt-nosed angels are depicted, the narrow loophole windows in the rough-cast wall, the square wooden tower, are all very much like the little church down by the Shaky Bridge; and Herman, not being archæologically given, does not desire to survey the interior of the fane. So they cross the churchyard, and go out of a little gate which brings them to a lane leading to nowhere in particular, a row of one-story cottages, thatched and in the last stage of decay, a forge, and a wooden building turned endways to the lane, which Herman supposes to be a dilapidated barn, until, looking up, he perceives a sign hanging from the angle nearest the road, and is thus made aware that it is 'The New Inn. M. A. Gredby. Licensed to sell beer, spirits, tobacco, &c.'

M. A. Gredby is one of Editha's pensioners; so Herman is introduced to the interior of the New Inn, which consists, or appears to consist, of the public room and a back kitchen. A corkscrew staircase squeezed into a corner suggests sleeping accommodation in the sloping roof. The public room is low and dark, the ceiling encumbered by timbers ponderous enough to sustain the upper chambers of a mediæval fortress. One side of the apartment is swallowed up by the open hearth and chimney; but, as M. A. Gredby's customers are in the habit of sitting in the chimney-corners, and making much of the fire even in summer-time, this is by no means lost space. Two old men in smock-frocks are seated on a bench inside the chimney to-day, smoking long clay pipes and looking at the fire.

The apartment, small in itself, and rendered smaller by its architectural characteristics, is farther reduced by an overplus of furniture—ancient high-backed windsor chairs, ponderous tables, and a horse-hair-covered sofa of clumsy proportions; garniture pendent from the cross-beams in the way of onions, bacon, and a netful of apples. The one latticed window is obscured by a variety of small wares designed to attract the eye of local childhood, but which seem to have missed their end, as the sugar-sticks have the pale and clouded look of advanced age, the hardbake has faded from brown to gray, the black-jack has oozed through its paper covering, and the battledores display more fly-marks than parchment.

Into this dark little den Herman peers wonderingly, while Mrs. Gredby pours forth her rapturous greeting. She is not a native of the district, and takes a pride in declaring the fact.

'To think that you should come to see me, Miss Editha, to-day of all days, and your wedding to-morrow! Yes, I saw it in the paper, and I means to walk over, if I drops on the way, to see you in your wedding-dress. And I've been trying to persuade my old gentleman; but, lor, he hasn't no spirit, he hasn't, and says he can't walk so far. He's a Welshman, you see, and he hasn't the spirit for it. I walks into Llandrysak and back again every market-day, and makes light of it, though I shall be sixty-five next birthday. But then I was born at Cheltenham; I don't belong to this place.'

Mrs. Gredby has lived at the New Inn for the last forty years, but has not yet got over her contempt for Llanmoel, which is only second in degree to her contempt for her old gentleman.

A grunt of acquiescence or negation from one of the old men smoking in the chimney-corner identifies him with the subject of Mrs. Gredby's discourse.

'Ah, you may grunt and grumble,' exclaims that lady, 'but if you had a hounce o' spirit, you'd walk over to Lochwithian to see Miss Editha in her wedding-dress.'

'I seed her father married,' mumbles the old man, without taking his pipe out of his mouth; 'that'll do for me. I seed her mother buried; that was a rare sight, that was—sixteen murning curches. That'll last my time. Miss has got my blessing wherever she goes; but I ain't got strength for no more sight-seeing.'

'I've brought Mr. Westray, the gentleman I'm going to marry, to see you,' says Editha.

'And a fine-grown gent he is too,' exclaims Mrs. Gredby; 'but, without offence to him, I wish he'd been Mr. Hetheridge. I'm no Welshwoman, thank God; if I was, I daresay I should take it more to heart that you're not going to marry a Welshman. But I do wish it had been Mr. Hetheridge—such a noble fresh-coloured young gentleman—and that you'd been going to settle among us.'

Editha blushes crimson, and Herman feels that his foot is not on his native heather, and that his name is a matter of indifference to Mrs. Gredby.

'Mr. Westray is a very famous gentleman in London,' says Editha; 'he writes books which people admire very much.'

'Tracks?' inquires Mrs. Gredby, somewhat scornfully.

'No, not tracts.'

'I'm glad of that. There's too many Methodies in this part of the country; they're always pestering with their blessed tracks. I likes my Bible as I likes my drop of spirits—neat. I don't care about having Scripture chopped into little bits and mixed up with other people's notions.'

'That reminds me, Mrs. Gredby, that I've brought you a Bible for a keepsake, and a couple of silver spoons for you and Mr. Gredby, so that you may think of me sometimes when you drink your tea.'

A small black teapot among the ashes on the hearth suggests that Mrs. Gredby is a confirmed tea-drinker.

'Bless your kind heart, miss, we don't want nothin' to remind us of you. We shall think of you often enough when you're settled up in London, which I'm told has growed into a very fine town, with a numbankmint and a wiadux, though not so genteel as my native place—Cheltenham. *We* shall think of you, Miss Editha, never fear.'

Editha extracts the Bible and the teaspoons from a variety of neat little packages in the basket. Both gifts are received with rapture, but it is clear that the teaspoons go nearest to Mrs. Gredby's heart. The Gredby initials—man and wife—have been engraved on each spoon.

'I never owned a silver teaspoon before, Miss Editha,' says the matron, 'though I come of a very respectable fambly. My mother had six teas and four salts, real silver, with King George and the leopard's head on them, besides a lion with his fore-pawr lifted up, and a deal of ornamentation; but my eldest brother came into them, with the rest of the property, as heir-at-law, and kep' 'em, set out among the glass and chaney on his cheffaneer, till things went wrong with him, being a master carpenter in a small way, and the spoons was murtgaged to his creditors.'

Mrs. Gredby's old gentleman crawls feebly out of

the chimney-corner to behold and admire the spoons, which he turns over in his horny palm as if they were natural curiosities.

After this it is time to say good-bye, and Mrs. Gredby dissolves into tears.

'I hope you wouldn't think it a liberty if I was to ask leaf to kiss you, Miss Editha, having knowd you from a child,' she says pathetically; and Editha submits to be kissed by the proprietress of the New Inn, who doesn't often taste butcher's meat—the nearest butcher living three miles off—and who makes up for that deprivation by a copious use of onions. Herman, suffering sympathetic torture, makes a wry face during the operation.

'And now,' says Mrs. Gredby, making a dart at the little black pot, 'you must have a cup o' tea and a bit of currant cake after your walk.'

Editha protests that she has not time to take refreshment, but the energetic M. A. Gredby snatches some cups and saucers from one of the numerous shelves which encumber the walls, and spreads them on a massive iron teatray. From another shelf she produces a mysterious-looking substance, of pallid hue, ornamented with black spots which look like defunct flies.

'It's a trifle mowldy, miss,' she apologises, as she slices this substance; 'but I made it with my own hands, and it's genuwine.'

Editha and Herman decline the cake on the ground of feeble appetite, but consent to take a little tea. That infusion is very black and very strong, and tastes so much like senna, that Herman is fearful lest Mrs. Gredby should be practising upon him for his ulterior benefit, after the manner of careful nurses with small children.

After making a faint pretence of drinking tea, Editha and her betrothed take leave of Mr. and Mrs. Gredby, and proceed to visit the smaller dwellings in the settlement. Everywhere Editha is received with the same tokens of affection, wept over, kissed, adored, while Herman stands looking on. It is sweet to him to see how much she is beloved, and his heart is stirred with a secret pride as he thinks how willingly she has surrendered all this worship and allegiance, her happy useful life among her native hills, to follow his uncertain fortunes.

The basket contains keepsakes for every one—always something pretty and useful and appropriate, which appears in every case to be the object most ardently desired by the recipient. Bright neckerchiefs, lace collars, Bibles, Testaments, inkstands, needlecases, come out of the basket, and elicit rapturous admiration.

'You'll not be forgotten when I am gone,' Editha tells her various pensioners; 'my sister will take care of you. You shall have your half-pound of tea every other Saturday the same as usual, Mrs. Davis.'

'It isn't that I'm thinking of, miss,' answers a hard-working matron. 'It's the sight of your bright face we shall miss.'

Llanmoel duly visited, Herman and Editha enter a lane—wild, rugged, and picturesque—which turns off at an angle by the side of the New Inn.

'Where are we going now?' asks Herman.

Editha points skyward.

'What, going to heaven so soon! I thought we were to be married first, and translated together.'

'I wish you wouldn't talk like that, Herman.

You see the bank yonder. We are going to a farm-house near the top.'

'I see a mountain, like Brighton racecourse turned up endways, dotted with sheep.'

'That's where we are going.'

'Do people live up there, for example?'

The lane is delightful—not always narrow; it widens by and by into a patch of wooded waste, with here and there a pool of water, fern-fringed, shadowed with blackberry and alder bushes, old hawthorns lichened and gray; all things wild, neglected, beautiful. Then the lane narrows again, and twists and wriggles up the hillside, and the valley widens as they rise above it; and Cymbries Bank and the Roman mound rise up before them far away to the west, in the glow of afternoon sunlight.

'Imagine anybody living up here,' cries Herman, 'alone among the Immensities, and nearly a day's journey from the butcher.'

Steeper and steeper grows the lane, screened with hazel-bushes and wild apple, hawthorn and elder, till it brings them into a triangular farmyard just under the summit of the hill. Such a lonely old farmhouse, decently kept and prosperous looking, the huge chimney-stacks composing about one-half of the building. A flight of steps leads up to the low wooden door, innocent of knocker or bell.

Herman thumps the portal with his stick, whereat a simple-minded-looking calf puts it head out of a shed in the yard and lows plaintively, and an unseen dog barks indignantly, but there is no other answer. Herman knocks again and again, but with no farther effect than irritating the invisible dog and puzzling the mild-faced calf, whose mother salutes the intruders with a resentful bellow.

'I daresay Maggie and Jenny have gone to Llandrysak,' says Editha. 'I should like to have seen them. They were my prize scholars three years ago, and the prettiest girls in the neighbourhood. Would you like to go to the top of the hill?'

'Having come so far, it would be dastardly to desist,' replies Herman. 'A friend of mine—a famous Alpine traveller in his way—told me that when he had got within twenty feet of the summit of Mont Blanc he would have given the world to lie down then and there, and give up life and the task together; but he crawled to the top somehow.'

They leave the farmyard by a narrow ledge which leads upward, and from the hilltop survey the world below, seated side by side upon a low stone wall, which for some unknown reason divides the summit. To the right and left of them are peaks as high as that they have climbed, one clothed with bracken, the other bare. Below them rushes a mountain torrent through the cloven hills. They can see the little wooden tower of Llanmoel church in the valley beneath, and far away in the clear blue the scattered white houses of Llandrysak; but of a human being, near or far, there is no sign.

'I can almost distinguish the Cambria, and Dewrance playing croquet,' says Herman.

Mr. Dewrance has come down to assist at to-morrow's ceremony. He has been succeeded at Llandrysak by a gentleman of an Evangelical turn, and the pretty little white and gray stone church on the common has made a retrograde movement, which is grateful to the native mind, but unwelcome to English visitors.

They sit for a little while curiously silent, moved to deepest thoughts by the serenity of the scene. On the threshold of her new life Editha's thoughts are mournful. Will he always love her, this stranger for whom she barters her nearest and dearest? Of Ruth's affection, of Ruth's sympathy, she is utterly sure; but his love may be a thing of impulse, and change or wane in the years to come. She looks at him wonderingly, fearfully, being certain of so little about him but the one absorbing truth that she loves him.

'Four o'clock, dearest, and we are between six and seven miles from the sound of the dressing-bell,' exclaims Herman, feeling that the melodious tinkling of a distant sheep-bell will speedily beguile him to slumber unless he bestirs himself somehow.

'We shall go home faster than we came, Herman; the way is almost all down-hill.'

'Ah, that's what makes the progress of life so rapid after five-and-twenty—it is all down-hill.'

They go back to the farmhouse. Herman assails the door with his stick again, and again in vain. But half-way down the lane they meet the farmer's daughters, dark-eyed, blooming, lovely, carrying heavy baskets, and delighted at the sight of Editha.

'I should have been so sorry if I'd gone away without seeing you, Maggie, and you too, Jenny.'

'O, if you please, miss, we are to be in the churchyard to-morrow with all your old scholars.'

'Really! That is kind.'

Maggie's and Jenny's keepsakes are fished out of the basket, and there are kisses and kindly words of farewell.

'That was a little better than being kissed by Mrs. Gredby,' says Herman, as he and Editha continue their journey.

'Poor Mrs. Gredby! When my brothers were little boys, it was their great delight to visit Mrs. Gredby, and sit in the chimney-corner with old Mr. Gredby. He used to make them pea-shooters, and to lend them an old gun long before they were allowed to have guns of their own. I'm afraid to think how much mouldy cake they must have eaten. I know Mrs. Gredby used to give them sausages, and black pudding, and all manner of dreadful things.'

'I daresay your Indian brother is suffering for those juvenile indiscretions now, and calling it liver,' replies Herman.

They arrive at Lochwithian only just in time for the dressing-bell. The Priory is full of guests. Editha's clerical brother has arrived on the scene, with his wife and two eldest girls, who are to be bridesmaids. Two young ladies of ancient Welsh family have come from a distant grange for the same purpose. Mr. Dewrance is there in readiness for to-morrow, and Mr. Petherick comes to dinner. Editha has no more time for mournful thoughts till late that night, when she kneels beside Ruth's sofa, and confides her vague doubts and fears to that sympathetic listener. Ruth's words are full of comfort.

'Dearest, your own heart has chosen,' she says. 'I think there is a divine instinct in a heart as pure and true as yours. Why should we fear the issue?'

'It seems so hard to leave you, Ruth, so selfish. But you do like him, don't you, Ruth? You can trust him?'

'Yes, dear; if he will only be true to the better part of his nature: and with you for his counsellor he can hardly be otherwise.'

To-morrow, and they stand side by side in the beautified church, before an altar glorious with all white flowers that bloom at this season—a church crowded with loving faces, many of them tearful, for at Lochwithian this marriage is in some wise a public calamity.

The autumn sun shines warm and bright. School-children, and young women who were Editha's scholars a few years ago, line the path from the church door to the Priory gates, and cast their tributary blossoms before the bridal pair. To young and old Editha, in her white dress and veil, seems like an angel.

The crowd does not lessen when the wedding party have gone back to the house; the people wait to see the last of their favourite. Mrs. Gredby is there, splendidly got up in a Paisley shawl of many colours and a green-gauze bonnet. There are two or three national hats come from remote villages, but smart bonnets of the last metropolitan fashion prevail.

There is to be a tea-drinking in the afternoon on a large scale for old and young, and in the mean time an itinerant vendor dispenses cakes and sweetstuff to the excited throng. At last the carriage which is to convey bride and bridegroom to the Llandrysak station appears before the porch, and, after an interval, Editha reappears in her simple travelling-dress, leaning on her father's arm, Herman on the other side, and the brother and sister-in-law, cousins, friends, and clergy in the background.

The young couple drive off amidst a burst of cheers which the hillsides echo thunderously, Editha looking back at her old home till the road winds and shuts it from her sight.

'Never quite my own home any more,' she murmurs sadly. 'Good-bye, happy days of youth!'

CHAPTER IV.

'Épouvantable et complet désastre. Le vaisseau sombrait sans laisser ni un cordage, ni une planche sur le vaste océan des espérances.'

THE Frivolity is closed during the season of London's emptiness, and Mrs. Brandreth is enjoying the blissfulness of repose at the sleepy little Belgian watering-place of Heldenberg, near the good old city of Memlingstadt. Not altogether a bad place, this Heldenberg, with its monster hotel and fine sea-wall; its vast stretch of golden sands and colony of bathing-boxes; its row of smart new villas facing the sea; and its cluster of ancient houses built in a snug little hollow under the lee of a sandbank, comfortably sheltered from ocean waves and stormy winds. There are the cosiest little restaurants down in this old town of Heldenberg, a sprinkling of humble shops, a dim old church, and a post-office. All the rest of Heldenburg is new, and spreads itself in a line with its face to the sea, steadfastly ignoring the original settlement, from whose abasement the fashionable watering-place is approached by steep stone steps, upon which shrill-voiced females exhibit their small wares, and tempt the idle visitor to unpremeditated outlay. Those large flat currant-cakes which are the glory of Belgium may be had here, and the Heldenberg mussel, a fish of some distinction, is purveyed upon the stone landings. Not often does the upper town descend to the lower town, the great hotel providing for all the wants of its patrons, internal and external, and the landscape between Heldenberg and Memlingstadt offering no farther attraction to the explorer than is to be found in level sands, intersected by an occasional ditch, or a row of stunted willows, a canal with barges and water-gates, and here and there the verdure of a cabbage-garden.

Mrs. Brandreth has come to Heldenberg as a quiet out-of-the-way place, where she is not likely to find many English people, or to be recognised and stared at. She has her reward. There are very few English at Heldenberg, which does not offer many attractions to the British mind. It is not a stage upon the high-road of Europe, like Ostend; it has no steamers, no direct communication with any place except Memlingstadt. Its *établissement* is infantine, its dissipations of the mildest order. The Belgians come here in flocks, proud of having created Heldenberg by their own unaided efforts. It is a plant of purely native growth, owes no favour to the rest of Europe, and its cleanliness, freshness, and brightness are very fair to Belgian eyes. To dress smartly, bathe abundantly, lounge away morning and afternoon on the esplanade, retiring at intervals for copious refreshment, and to hear indifferent music and play small games of chance in the evening, make up the sum of life at Heldenberg; a placid simple existence, not over-costly, and leaving no bad taste in the mouth.

Myra has brought a box of new books, and a point-lace flounce, which she has been at work upon for the last three years. She has avoided the public life of the monster hotel, enjoyable as it is to Belgian visitors, and has established herself in two pretty rooms, *au premier*, in one of the villas facing the sea. A large family of healthy-looking children, whose existence appears to be one perpetual mealtime, occupy the apartments beneath. Myra has a balcony, lattice-shaded, in which she can sit on warm afternoons reading or working, or studying her part in Herman's new comedy, which work of genius he placed in her hands a few days before his last journey to Radnorshire.

The piece is strong, full of domestic interest and telling situations, and Myra's part is one of the finest she has ever had written for her. This quiet Belgian watering-place affords her ample leisure for study. She has time to think out the character; to create a living breathing woman from the words of her author; to enlarge upon his ideas, and give form to his airiest fancy.

'I think even he will be proud and pleased if I carry out my idea of the character,' she says to herself, sitting in the balcony in the warm afternoon sunshine with the manuscript comedy on her lap, just two days after Herman's wedding.

She has thought herself remote from all her world, and has been luxuriating in the rest and freedom which accompany the thought, when looking idly down at the esplanade she sees a gentleman in gray, with a white hat and hay-coloured whiskers, steadfastly regarding the balcony. He lifts his hat as she looks at him, and reveals the somewhat commonplace features of Lord Earlswood.

'How do you do, Mrs. Brandreth?' he remarks, with his accustomed tranquillity. 'I thought I couldn't be mistaken. Your people could not tell me your number, so I have been exploring What's-its-name. I forget what the Belgians call this settlement. Rather like the east-end of Margate without the cockneys, isn't it?'

'Pray come in, if you want to talk,' says Myra, with vexation of spirit, rolling up her manuscript.

Lord Earlswood is prepared to converse placidly from the pavement, regardless of the impression he may make upon the various families which crowd the brand-new villas.

'May I?' he says. 'So delighted!'

He ascends the stone steps, disappears through the open portal, and reappears in Myra's drawing-room, where the new books are scattered on sofa and tables, and the point-lace flounce displays itself half in and half out of a fairy work-basket lined with quilted rose-coloured satin. The newly-furnished apartment looks like a scene on the stage.

'How do you do?' says Myra, stifling a yawn. She had been in a delicious reverie that was almost slumber when her listless gaze alighted on Lord Earlswood's white hat. 'What brings you to this quiet little place?'

'You may well ask that. I think it would have been only friendly to let a fellow know where you were coming. I called in Bloomsbury-square. No one could tell me anything, except that you'd gone to some foreign watering-place. It might be Ostend, or Boulogne, or Dieppe, or Biarritz, or Arcachon, or Jericho—no one knew. Went to the theatre—same result: meeting of the company announced for the 6th of October—that was all. It was Mrs. Lockstitch, your wardrobe woman, who put me on the right scent. She had made your dresses, and you had told her you wanted them in a quiet style for a quiet place. Hel—something, in Belgium. I looked up *Murray*, and found only one Belgian watering-place beginning with Hel; and here I am. Clever, wasn't it?'

'Pertinacious, at any rate,' replies Myra.

'Ah, that's the next best thing, if it isn't better. "It's doggedness does it." I came across that sentence somewhere the other day, and it took my fancy. I flatter myself there's a good deal of doggedness in my composition.'

'I thought you were grouse-shooting in the Highlands?'

'Everybody shoots grouse; I don't.'

'You must be very anxious about your theatre,' says Myra, taking up her flounce, and doing a stitch or two, *point Turque*, with infinite precision.

'I don't care two straws about the theatre. Come, Mrs. Brandreth, you know that as well as I do. I built it for you, just as I might have sent you a box of bonbons on New Year's-day.'

'A princely *bonbonnière*. But I am glad Fortune has been kind, and that so far you have had interest for your money.'

'It's not very friendly to talk in that business-like way when a fellow has come across from Dover to Ostend—the worst passage I ever made—on purpose to see you.'

'Extremely kind on your part, but rather foolish; unless Heldenberg and the Belgians prove amusing enough to reward your devotion. What can you have to say to me, or I to you, that would not be just as well said a month hence?'

'I don't know about that. First and foremost, I came to see you. It's a pleasure to me even to sit here watching you stitching at that blue-calico-and-white-tape arrangement. And then, again, I've a little bit of news for you,' he adds, with a faint sparkle in his dull gray eyes. 'News that I thought might interest you—about a friend of ours.'

'What kind of news?' asks Myra, working industriously to cure her sleepiness.

'Well, I should call it—matrimonial.'

'Miss Belormond has had an offer from that sporting baronet with the tight legs who used to hang about the stage-door?'

'No.'

'Mr. Flanders, the low comedian, has married Bella Walters—at last? I'm sure she has tried hard enough to bring it about, poor girl!'

'No.'

'Then I give it up.'

'Your friend, Mr. Westray—' begins Lord Earlswood slowly.

The work drops from Myra's hands as she looks up at him.

'Well, what of him?'

'O, nothing very particular. His marriage is in yesterday's *Times*.'

'Some other Westray, perhaps.'

'No; Herman Westray. Here's the paper;' and his lordship produces a neatly-folded supplement. 'Herman Westray, only son of the late Reverend Thomas Westray of Colehaven, Devon, to Editha, second daughter of Morgan Morcombe, Esq., Lochwithian Priory, Radnorshire.'

'I rather expected it,' says Myra, with heroic composure. 'I have seen them together at the Frivolity.'

'O,' exclaims Earlswood, mortified, 'then you're not surprised?'

'Not particularly. If you crossed the Channel with the idea that you were bringing me a piece of astounding news, you have wasted your trouble.'

She is especially gracious to him after this; allows him to share her afternoon tea, discusses her plans for the coming season at the Frivolity, and dismisses him in the last stage of mystification. And by and by, alone in her pretty bedchamber, with its snow-white drapery and continental gimcrackery, she falls on her knees and raises her clasped hands, and takes an awful oath—not to the God of the Christians assuredly, who can hardly be supposed to receive such vows, but to Nemesis, or the three fatal spinsters who deal calamity to man.

CHAPTER V.

> 'We'll live together like two neighbour vines,
>   Circling our souls and loves in one another.
> We'll spring together, and we'll bear one fruit;
> One joy shall make us smile, and one grief mourn;
> One age go with us, and one hour of death
>   Shall close our eyes, and one grave make us happy.'

HERMAN's honeymoon fleets past him like a blissful dream. Life, which he had thought worn out and done with, save as a mere mechanical process, seems to have begun afresh for him—life and youth and happiness all renewed together like a second birth. Editha's companionship is so sweet in its utter novelty. This pure heart has so many treasures to lay at his feet. This innocent mind has such unknown deeps for him to sound. As her lover he had fancied that he knew all the wealth of her nature. As her husband he discovers a new world of thought and feeling which the girl had veiled from him.

Too fleet, too fair are those early days of their

wedded life; like those radiant mornings which are apt to end in dull weather, the rose changing to gray, the sun vanishing behind angry clouds.

They have no thought of such change, these wedded lovers. Editha has no longer any doubt as to the wisdom of her choice, or the possibility of perfect happiness in this imperfect world. She sits by her husband one night while he writes a chapter of his novel, watches all the lights and shadows of the mobile face which changes with his theme, and is beyond measure happy. It is as if she had actually a part in his work, in his thoughts, in his genius; and when he reads her the concluded chapter—ineffable condescension!—bliss beyond the power of language to express.

She writes to Ruth from a little Swiss village, a letter brimming over with joy, one of those honeymoon letters which we all receive occasionally from sister, or cousin, or familiar friend; a letter in which every sentence begins with 'Dear Herman,' 'Dear Herman thinks,' 'Dear Herman says,' 'Dear Herman hopes,'—a letter which illustrates all the weaknesses of woman, and all her virtues.

That bright month—not to be reckoned as other months in the calendar—comes to an end like a tale that is told, and the newly-married couple come home to the house at Fulham. Then come new pleasures, the simple joys of domesticity. Huge chests of linen, sent up from Lochwithian Priory, to be unpacked and put away. Wedding presents to be disposed judiciously about the rooms; no easy task, as these gifts are for the most part incongruous and of doubtful taste—a pink-and-gold French clock and candelabra, for instance, which are an eyesore in that perfect drawing-room, whose pale green and white and tender lilacs are as delicate as a picture by Greuze.

Editha is enchanted with her new home. There is an artistic grace about the river-side villa, with its light airy rooms. Not numerous, but of a fair size. Messrs. Molding and Korness, not being harassed by interference from their customer, have surpassed themselves. There is nothing costly, or that strikes the observer as costly; no gilding, except the slenderest line of unburnished gold here and there; no sheen of satin or splendour of brocade; no vast expanse of looking-glass, confusing the sense with imaginary space. The Pompeian vestibule and dining-room are deliciously simple; encaustic tiles, unpolished ebony, cretonne draperies of classic design and rich subdued colour. The walls are painted a delicate French gray, relieved by a four-foot dado of ebonised panelling, and the ceiling of palest primrose. A broad border of ebonised wood surrounds the Venetian glass over the chimneypiece, and on this broad framework there are brackets supporting small bronze figures which might have been dug out of the lava that buried Herculaneum. A cretonne curtain divides the dining-room from a smaller chamber, looking upon the somewhat dingy byroad by which the villa is approached. This room has been lined from floor to ceiling on two sides with ebonised shelves for the accommodation of Herman's library, which is rather of the future than the present, his existing collection filling about a third of the space Messrs. Molding and Korness have allowed him; his desk, his reading-lamp, his chair, are perfection of their kind. A sofa of classic design has been provided for Editha opposite her husband's writing-table; a stand with russia-leather portfolio suggests a collection of photographs, which may help her to while away an idle hour; a rustic work-table in a corner hints at stocking-mending and the sewing-on of shirt-buttons. Glass, china, all the details of housekeeping are in harmony with one pervading idea. Everything is artistic. The very beer-jugs are Etrurian; the urn is as purely Greek as that finely sculptured brazen vase from which Antigone poured her libation upon the dead.

The servants have been provided by the house-agent, and have been recommended as models of probity. They are cook, housemaid, and parlour-maid, and present a very fair appearance on the evening of Mr. and Mrs. Westray's arrival, congregated in the hall to carry in the boxes and travelling-bags—three smartly-dressed young women, whose starched muslin aprons are their only badge of servitude.

Now Editha begins her duties as matron and housekeeper, and all the small troubles and vexations of housekeeping on a limited scale gradually reveal themselves to her. After their first breakfast at home, when the rooms, and the cups and saucers, and the view from the windows, and the servants' faces are still as new to them as if they had just put up at a strange hotel, Herman gives his young wife twenty pounds and the daintiest little morocco account-book ever devised to make accounts fascinating.

'I think it will be wisest to pay the bills weekly, dear,' he says, 'and then we shall always know exactly how we stand financially. Do you think twenty pounds is enough for you to begin with?'

'O Herman, twenty pounds ought to last us ever so long; a month I should think. Twenty pounds used to last a long time at Lochwithian, though we had ten servants instead of three. Certainly papa paid all the large accounts quarterly, and we had a great deal from the home farm.'

'Here you will have to pay for everything. Bridge-end House produces nothing, not so much as a sprig of parsley to decorate the butter.'

On this first day Herman leaves his wife to face the responsibilities of her position alone. He has been away from London five weeks, and is anxious to see his publishers, to look in at his favourite club, and to ascertain in a general way how the world has wagged in his absence. Editha goes to the hall-door with him, and sees him depart with that faint touch of heart-sinking which young wives are subject to on such occasions. Throughout their honeymoon they have not lived an hour asunder. This is the beginning of stern reality. Editha lingers in the hall for a minute or two, contemplating the rather dull outlook from the window: a dwarfed hedgerow and level market-garden stretching away towards Walham Green; a church-spire and gray housetops in the distance; not so much as a mound of earth to relieve the dismal flatness of a cabbage and asparagus producing world. Then she screws her courage to the sticking-place, and penetrates those hidden and rearward premises of which she is nominal mistress, thinking that for this first day it will be wise to go to the cook, instead of summoning that functionary to an interview.

It is eleven o'clock by this time, and Mrs. Westray finds her establishment at luncheon, seated comfortably at the kitchen table with a substantial upstanding wedge of double gloucester, a quartern loaf, and the largest of the Etrurian beer-jugs before them.

They look somewhat disconcerted by her appearance, which they evidently regard as an intrusion. Cook wipes her mouth hastily and rises. She is a young woman, buxom and florid, with a look of having developed her figure upon buttered toast and hot suppers—a young woman with a sensual under-lip and a cunning eye. Housemaid and parlour-maid keep their seats. Very different this from Editha's welcome in the great old-fashioned kitchen at Lochwithian, where the cook and housekeeper of twenty years' service worshipped her, and the Welsh maidens smiled and curtsied as at the coming of a princess.

She discusses the dinner question. First, as the most important, cook has made bold to order the kitchen dinner already, to avoid loss of time. A nice little loin of pork and apple dumplings. 'The others like pork,' she says, with an air of self-abnegation. For the late dinner she suggests a pair of soles, a pair of fowls, and a small ham.

'Which Fullers the tea-grocer says he has some prime York 'ams at sixteenpence a pound, and I might make you a happle tart, mum, and a few custards.'

This dinner, though fair enough as a sample of the cook's capabilities, does not appear strikingly novel to Editha. Their honeymoon dinners have run very much upon roast fowl in those out-of-the-way Swiss hotels.

She racks her brains in the endeavour to think of something else; but saddles of mutton, fillets of veal, and fore-quarters of lamb are the only ideas that present themselves to her mind, and these are inappropriate to a *tête-à-tête* dinner.

'I think Mr. Westray would like a little game,' she hazards.

'You might have a brace of pheasants, mum, after the fowls.'

Four winged creatures to dine two people! There seems something wrong here.

'I should think one fowl and one pheasant would be quite enough,' says the young housekeeper.

'It might be *enough*, ma'am, but it wouldn't

do credit to a gentleman's table; and if master should 'appen to bring 'ome a friend promiscuous, the dinner would look shabby; and I'm sure you wouldn't wish that—just at first too.'

'No, of course I don't wish that.'

So cook has her way, and Editha feels somehow that this first attempt is not good housekeeping; and yet she has kept her father's house with credit and renown from seventeen years of age upwards, has dealt out stores on a large and liberal scale, kept accounts, and been nominally mistress of everything.

But it is one thing to deal with old servants whose master's goods are as their own—who would shudder at the idea of diverting a loaf of bread or a basin of dripping from its proper use; who are as proud of the family they serve and as anxious for the family credit as if the same blood flowed in their veins, and the same good old race made honour a necessity of their being—and to have commerce with these sharp-witted London-bred girls, who look upon every new household they enter as a caravansera which they can leave at their pleasure, and domestic service as a means to the one great end of their existence, which includes good living, fine dress, and evenings out.

After her interview with the cook, Editha surveys the parlour-maid's pantry, which Messrs. Molding and Korness have made as perfect as a steward's cabin on board a modern steamship, but which the young person who has charge of it pronounces dark and damp.

'And I'm afraid we shall be overrun with mice, ma'am, for I've heard them scuffling after dark. I suppose it's along of living so near the river,' adds the damsel, with a suppressed shudder.

The storeroom and china-closet are in one, filled with locked presses for linen and groceries. In one of these presses Editha and the two maids stow away the ample supply of house-linen, the making and marking of which, by the school-children of Lochwithian, it has been Ruth's pride to supervise. The grocery-closet Editha discovers will be useless, as the grocer calls every day for orders; and the cook assures her that it will be best and cheapest to order everything as it is wanted.

'I don't believe grocery would keep in them cupboards, mum, so near the river,' adds cook sagaciously; whereat Editha begins to understand that Father Thames is a friend to mice and inimical to grocery.

The grocery question settled, Mrs. Westray informs her household that she intends to pay all bills weekly, except such occasional supplies as can be paid for with ready money. She declares furthermore that she will require all accounts to be carefully examined and errors noted before they are submitted to her.

The cook seems somewhat to disapprove of weekly payments; her last master paid everything by cheque, half-yearly, she informs Editha, and evidently considers her last master's method the nobler of the two.

'But if you do intend to pay weekly, mum,' adds Jane the cook, with a sigh, 'there's a few little accounts I'd better give you at once.'

She searches a sauce-tureen or two and a vegetable-dish, which vessels contain reels of cotton, old letters, a dirty collar, small change, penholders, and various oddments appertaining to the three young persons who are good enough to accept a temporary shelter in Mrs. Westray's house. From one of these receptacles she produces half a dozen crumpled bills more or less greasy; and from these documents Editha discovers that the week preceding her arrival—during which the young persons have been settling down in their new service, and making believe to clean rooms which had never been soiled—has been a somewhat expensive period. There is a little bill from the baker, and a hieroglyphical paper from the butcher, the original obscurity of which has been made more obscure by grease. Eitha just contrives to decipher that the young persons have consumed three shoulders of mutton and four loins of pork in the week, and that they have furthermore required suet and calves' liver. The grocer's bill is the most alarming, for the grocer is a monopolist in his way, and sells bacon, cheese, eggs, and butter, as well as tallow-chandlery and colonial produce. Blacklead, bathbrick, sweet oil, hearthstone, scouring-paper, housemaids' gloves, lucifer matches, gas tapers, brooms, brushes, and blacking mount up in a positively awful manner. Six pounds and three-quarters of bacon have been indispensable as a provision for the four transparent rashers served at that morning's breakfast; nine pounds elveven ounces of double gloucester have been necessary to start the kitchen, and half a stilton has been ordered for the dining-room. Tea, coffee, sugar, rice, and tapioca have been laid in with equal liberality. There will be very little change out of a five-pound note from Mr. Fullers the grocer. Altogether Editha finds that her first payments will swallow up half of Herman's twenty pounds, and she has the satisfaction of hearing from the housemaid that more brooms, brushes, turksheads, furniture polishes, and Brunswick blacks are required before the house can be cleaned in a satisfactory manner.

This investigation of domestic affairs occupies some time, and then Editha goes up to her own pretty rooms and begins the task of unpacking. She has no maid—having insisted upon dispensing with that luxury in her new life, and being at all times independent of help—so the unpacking and arrangement of the trousseau takes a long time; so long that she has but a few minutes to write hurriedly to Ruth, announcing her establishment in her new home.

'You must come to me soon, darling,' she writes, 'if Dr. Price thinks you can bear the journey. I long so to see you, to tell you all about our Swiss tour, and how more than good dear Herman is. I feel rather strange and lonely to-day in my new home, dear Herman having been obliged to go to town on business—about his new book, you know, dear. It seems so odd to see strange servants, instead of the kind friendly faces at Lochwithian. I have brought presents for all of them from Switzerland, which I shall send in the box with your clock and jewel-casket; the clock from me, the casket from Herman, his own choice. I think you will like the carving.'

After this letter has been written and despatched, the day seems rather to hang upon Editha's hands. The house, pretty as it is, has that new look which is not quite friendly. The impress of Messrs. Molding and Korness's work is still upon it—the varnish too bright, the colours of the draperies too fresh. Editha cannot feel that it is home yet a while; and then this first severance from Herman even for a few hours is a trial. By five o'clock in the afternoon he seems to have been away so long. She wonders that he has not contrived to settle all business matters, and come back in time to take her for a walk before dusk.

She goes into the garden, but on this dull October afternoon Father Thames looks gloomy. A fog obscures the Surrey shore. A street-lamp, lighted too soon, shows dimly here and there among the cold gray houses. Everything is dull and cold. She walks up and down the gravel-path by the water, and looks over the low boundary at a wide reach of mud despondently, and wonders to find that so large a portion of this much-extolled river consists of a dark slimy filth, obnoxious to sight and smell.

She soon wearies of that narrow lawn and gravel-path, so different from the gardens at Lochwithian, and goes back to the house, where she tries to amuse herself by looking at Herman's library. This does not prove particularly interesting, being confined to books of reference, admirable in their way, and those standard works with which Editha is familiar. She takes out a volume of Goldsmith's *Citizen of the World*, and tries to read; but her thoughts wander from the page, and she finds herself listening for Herman's return.

They are to dine at half-past seven. At six the parlour-maid brings her a wishy-washy cup of tea, and a thin slice of new bread thickly buttered. This refreshment fails to revive her spirits, and she finds herself lapsing into melancholy on this first day of her home life.

But at last, just as she comes down-stairs in her simple dinner dress, a latchkey sounds in the hall-door, and Herman appears. Happy meeting, fond welcome, as after a severance of years.

'Why, my love, you look pale and tired,' he says, as they go into the library together. 'You haven't been over-exerting yourself about domestic duties, I hope?'

'O no, dear; only—'

'Only what, my pet?'

'The day has seemed so long and dull without you.'

'Has it, darling?' he exclaims, pleased by the avowal. 'I oughtn't to have gone to town the first day, perhaps; only I was anxious to see Standish about my novel, and to hear what had been doing in the last six weeks. You went for a walk, I hope, dear?'

'What alone, Herman, in this strange place!'

'Ah, to be sure—you don't know the neighbourhood yet. There are some nice walks—Barnes Common, for instance, not above half an hour's walk from here; and Wimbledon, almost as near; I must show you them next week. And now I'll go and wash my hands for dinner. I've eaten no lunch, on purpose to do justice to our first home dinner.'

'I hope it will be nice, dear; but the cook is rather young. However, she seems to understand things, and is very confident.'

The table in the Pompeian chamber looks pretty enough, with the fragile modern glass and heavy old silver—the last the Squire's gift to his daughter —when Herman and his wife go in to dinner presently; but the dinner itself is a failure, and Herman resents the fact more intensely than Editha would have expected from a poet.

The soles are burned on the outside and pink within; the fowls are the oldest and toughest birds Herman has encountered for some time, and Swiss poultry has not been always young; the ham is half raw, hard, and salt; the pheasants are reduced to a condition in which the flesh crumbles off their bones; the bread-sauce is watery; the gravy is chiefly remarkable for grease, Lee and Perrin, and black pepper; the pastry is a leaden sarcophagus, in which a few half-cooked apples are entombed; the custards are curdled. But happily, before they arrive at this stage of the feast, Herman has spoiled an excellent appetite with a series of disappointments, and has retired within himself.

O, those nice little club dinners—so simple, so inexpensive! The one whiting, crisp and of a golden brown, with his tail in his mouth—delicate symbol of eternity; the longitudinal slice of haunch, roasted by a cook who has elevated roasting to a science. Herman is not so practical as to count the cost of this first home dinner, or he would find the account sadly against domesticity.

Soles	.	.	.	.	.	.	£0 2 6
Fowls	.	.	.	.	.	.	0 7 6
Ham	.	.	.	.	.	.	0 13 7½
Pheasants	.	.	.	.	.	.	0 8 0
Gravy-beef, vegetables, eggs, butter, lard, and sundries	.	.	.	.	.	.	0 5 0
Total	.	.	.	.	.	.	£1 16 7½

His dinner at the club would have cost him three-and-sixpence; but then he cannot take Editha to a club, and it is an established principle in the British mind that to dine out of doors is adverse to the best interests of domestic life.

'I am afraid you have not enjoyed your dinner, dear,' Editha says nervously, when the parlour-maid, who is slow and stately in her movements, has swept the last crumb from the tablecloth, and withdrawn her attentive ear from Mr. and Mrs. Westray's conversation.

'We won't call it dinner, Editha. Everything was simply uneatable. You must tell your cook so to-morrow; and if she can't do better, you must dismiss her. There must be plenty of good cooks to be had, if you go the right way to work.'

Editha sighs. It seems a bad beginning somehow, insignificant as the matter is to her mind. Herman drinks a couple of glasses of claret, conquers a disposition towards ill-temper, and they retire to the pretty little study, where there is a cheery fire on this dull October evening, and sit opposite each other on either side of the hearth like old-established married people, and Editha is happy again.

They talk and talk, having such a boundless stock of ideas to impart to each other, that there seems no limit to the possibility of interesting conversation. Herman expounds his views upon a variety of subjects; vague dreamy views, tricked out in a halo of sentiment. He tells his wife a little about his day in London; the people he has met, the news he has heard; not altogether edifying.

'I'm afraid it is a very wicked world you hear of at the clubs, Herman,' she says, shocked to learn that A.'s wife has run away with a Queen's Messenger; that there is a rumour of a judicial separation between Mr. and Mrs. B.; that C., after *menant grand train* for the last three years, has appeared in the *Gazette;* that D. has levanted on account of some unknown difficulty, which may be anything from flirtation to forgery.

'It is the best world we know of, my dear,' he answers calmly; 'and we can but make the best of it; get the most out of it; give it the least; trust it never; hope for little from its generosity; for nothing from its charity; and be sure that he who has the biggest mote in his own eye will be the first to spot the beam in ours. Yes, it is a wicked world undoubtedly, and, unluckily for the cause of morality, the wicked people in it are the pleasantest companions and do the kindest things.'

'You don't mean what you say, Herman!' exclaims his wife, horrified.

'Some of it, at any rate, dearest,' he answers carelessly. 'But I don't want to infect your innocent soul with my time-hardened notions. The world you know is fair enough—that smooth-faced, time-serving world which smiles upon the prosperous and well-placed. God forbid that you should ever test its metal with the acid of misfortune, or discover how the fine gold changes to dross in the crucible of adversity!'

Editha sighs. Worldly wisdom like this seems chilling after Ruth's gentle views of life, overflowing with hopefulness and charity.

'I think if you were to give me a good cup of tea, Editha, I might manage a chapter or two to-night,' says Herman, after a pause, during which he has been looking dreamily at the fire, and tasting the sweets of domesticity. It is sweet to him to sit by his own fireside, with Editha opposite him—to know that she is absolutely his own.

The young wife is delighted at that demand for tea. She rings, and the stately parlour-maid stalks in presently with the urn and caddy, the old-fashioned silver tea-tray, part of Editha's dower, and rosebud cups and saucers; and Editha is prettily busy for the next five minutes, while Herman goes on dreaming. His new book will be a success; his wife's delight in the chapters he has read to her seems to him a good augury. His comedy has been received with rapture by Mrs. Brandreth and her company, and only awaits the seal of public favour. Life smiles upon him as it has never smiled yet.

He has not seen Myra since his return to England. He has had some thoughts of calling at the theatre to-day, his piece being already in rehearsal; but he has shrunk somehow from the notion of his first encounter with Mrs. Brandreth in his character of married man, and has deferred his appearance at the Frivolity till to-morrow, or possibly the day after, or perhaps next week; although he is quite aware that such postponement may result in one or two of his characters working out into something utterly alien to his idea of them, and some of his best speeches being in a manner read backwards.

'I'll write to Myra to-morrow, just to let her know that I have returned, and to give her my new address,' he thinks.

He is anxious about his comedy, but it would be a relief to him if his comedy could succeed without any meeting between him and Mrs. Brandreth.

Kismet is the name of the new play. Modern, domestic, and so far original that its author is unconscious of having borrowed anybody else's ideas.

The cup of tea is perfection, and in sipping that brain-clearing beverage Herman forgets that he has had a bad dinner. He talks of his book; his characters, and that awful crisis in their fates which now looms before him in the middle of the third volume; and thoroughly enjoys himself for the next half-hour. And then the tea-tray is removed, the Sutherland table folded and put away, and the author seats himself at his desk; while Editha opens her work-basket, and concentrates her attention upon point-lace, or seems so to do, though after every group of stitches she looks up from her work, and watches the thoughtful face of the writer.

By and by she takes a volume of Coleridge—the Aldine edition, portable, clear of type—from Herman's classic bookshelf, and reads. Seated thus, with Herman opposite her, she knows no weariness, though she has read nearly to the end of the volume before the writer looks up from his manuscript at the sound of the silver-tongued clock on the mantelpiece striking two.

'My dearest, what have I been doing to allow you to stay up so long?' he exclaims. 'Your roses will soon fade if you keep me company in the small hours.'

'Let me stay, Herman,' she pleads. 'I am as foolish as David Copperfield's Dora, and I should be glad if I could hold your pens. It is so sweet to me to look up from my book now and then and watch your face, and fancy that I can follow the progress of your story there. Will you read me what you have just written?'

'Not to-night, love,' with a yawn. 'You shall read it for yourself in the printer's slips, and tell me the blemishes in my work. And now, wife of mine, I wonder whether your domestic handiness would go far enough to give me a b.-and-s.?'

The obedient wife flies to the cellaret; and for the first time in her life Squire Morcombe's daughter opens a soda-water bottle.

CHAPTER VI.

'Etait-ce un connaisseur en maitère de femme,
Cet écrivain qui dit que, lorsqu'elle sourit,
Elle vous trompe, elle a pleuré toute la nuit?'
　　　*　　　*　　　*　　　*　　　*
Je ne sais si jamais l'éternelle justice
A du plaisir des dieux un plaisir permis;
Mais, s'il m'était donné de dire à quel supplice
Je voudrais condamner mon plus fier ennemi,
C'est toi, pâle souci d'une amour dédaignée,
Désespoir misérable et qui meurs ignoré,
Oui, c'est toi, ce serait ta lame empoisonnée,
Que je voudrais briser dans un cœur abhorré!'

Kismet has been in rehearsal a fortnight before Herman makes his first appearance on the dimly-lighted stage, where the actors are endeavouring to give form and life to his creations, and to infuse some touch of novelty into those well-worn types which the dramatic writer is fain to employ, for want of power to evolve any new order of being from his inner consciousness.

Mrs. Brandreth is on the stage, rehearsing without book, in that low repressed tone with which she keeps feeling and passion in check, reserving her great effects—her fire and force and whirlwind of passion—for the performance. No one ever quite knows what 'Brandreth' is going to do till the first night of the new piece; perhaps Brandreth herself least of all. Artist though she is, and carefully as she thinks out and elaborates every character, she is not the less spontaneous. Some of her finest touches of art have come to her at night, before her audience, in a flash, like inspiration. Every movement of the graceful form, every turn of the small classic head, has been studied with deliberation. Yet at the last moment hidden fires flame out, and she electrifies her fellow-actors by some unpremeditated look or action which nothing less than genius could inspire.

Lord Earlswood sits across a chair, his arms folded on the back of it, his chin reposing on his arms, his whiskers drooping languidly. This is the fifth time he has assisted at the rehearsal of *Kismet*. His presence is an infliction which would be tolerated from no less a person than the owner of the theatre. He looks up as Herman comes to the wing, nods, and smiles thoughtfully, with a quick glance at Myra, who, with figure drawn to its fullest height, and scornfully uplifted head, is denouncing the weak-minded lover who has jilted her, loving her all the while, but sacrificing love to worldly wisdom.

His lordship looks from the author to the actress, wondering how they will meet. He has not seen them together since the Ascot Cup-day, when their evident enjoyment of each other's society galled him considerably. He has long ago made up his mind that there is something more than friendship in Myra's regard for the companion of her girlish years, and he is anxious to see how she will take Mr. Westray's marriage. She received the news of it coolly enough, it is true, much to Lord Earlswood's surprise; but then women are so artful, and have such wondrous self-command. The actual presence of the faithless one may be more trying.

The act ends with that outburst of Myra's. Despite her suppressed tones there is a force in her utterance and a meaning in her gestures which thrill the small audience watching her from the wing; and a little burst of spontaneous applause heralds the climax which is to bring down the curtain triumphantly upon act two.

'That licks *Hemlock*, anyhow,' says Lord Earlswood approvingly. 'Hang your classical rot! We had enough of that at Eton. We don't go to the theatre to be reminded of our juvenile canings and impositions. There's human interest here, passion, and what's-its-name? How d'ye do, Westray?'

At sound of the name Myra looks round. Pale, wearied with a three hours' rehearsal, she has been for ever so long. If her cheek blanches now, the change is so slight as to escape even the watchful eye of jealousy glancing gloomily upward from beneath the bent brows of Lord Earlswood.

'At last!' exclaims Mrs. Brandreth, as she and Herman shake hands. 'I began to think that some one else must have written *Kismet,* and that you had only given us the use of your name for a consideration. You seem to take so little interest in the piece.'

'I knew I was in good hands,' says Herman.

'He was "married, and couldn't come." Haw!' cries his lordship.

'How much of the rehearsal have you heard?' asks Mrs. Brandreth.

'Only the last half-dozen speeches. Nothing could be better. You will be magnificent in the close of that act. How d'ye do, Miss Belormond?' acknowledging that young lady's nods and becks and wreathed smiles.

'How well you are looking!' says Myra, in her friendliest manner; a frankly gracious friendliness that is new to Herman, and which relieves him of certain anxieties that have made this first visit to the Frivolity in some wise a trial. 'Switzerland has agreed with you. You look ten years younger than on that delightful day at Ascot.'

'And yet I was very happy on that day,' replies Herman, moved to gallantry by her kindness. A married man has such an agreeable sense of freedom. He can say the sweetest things with impunity.

'I think we might call the third act for tomorrow,' interjects the stage-manager, a gentleman who wears spectacles and his hat tilted on to the back of his head, and has an oppressed and careworn countenance, as of one whose burden is greater than he can bear.

'Yes,' replies Myra; 'the first and second go pretty smoothly now.'

'Mr. Scruto wants to show you his model for the second act,' adds the stage-manager, ' if you're not in a hurry to go.'

The rehearsal is over, but the actors linger, curious to hear anything that Herman may have to say; not that they intend to accept his ideas, good, bad, or indifferent, having already made up their minds as to their interpretation of his play.

Herman and Myra talk over the comedy, while Lord Earlswood swings backwards and forwards on his chair, and Mr. Delmaine, the stage-manager, roams about distractedly, bawling some direction or question now and then at one of the wings or up to the flies, whence come hoarse answering shouts from invisible sources. Herman's spirits have risen wonderfully since he came in at the stage-door. He discusses his play with vivacity, suggests a good deal, yet avows his supreme confidence in Myra's taste and experience.

They talk of the piece, and nothing but the piece, for some time, and then, having quite exhausted that subject, Myra says, in a subdued tone:

'I must not forget to offer you my congratulations on your marriage. I saw Miss Morcombe with you one night when we were playing *Hemlock*. She is very lovely. You have reason to be proud of her.'

'I am proud of her,' answers Herman. 'She is as good as she is beautiful.'

'You will let me know her some day, I hope.'

'I shall be very glad,' replies Herman; although half an hour ago he would have deemed such an introduction the wildest imprudence. 'She is already one of your most enthusiastic admirers, though she has only seen you once.'

'I saw how much she was interested in the play,' says Mrs. Brandreth; 'but I put that down to her interest in the author.'

'You did not know—'

'No, but I could see.'

Hereupon arrives Mr. Scruto the scene-painter, with his neat little cardboard model of the set for act two. Nothing can be more perfect in its way. It represents the garden of a villa at Nice, with the sunlit sea beyond, and an angle of the villa occupying one side of the foreground. The open windows reveal the pretty *salon* within, and in and out of these windows the *dramatis personæ* are to circulate.

Mr. Scruto's work is praised, a suggestion or two made by Mr. Delmaine, and approved by Mrs. Brandreth, and then the whole business of rehearsal is over. The prompter's boy puts up the call for to-morrow:

Kismet, act three, at 11.
Ladies of the Ballet.

Which latter announcement means that guests are to meander in and out during the last scene of the play. Mrs. Brandreth has a knack of training her ballet ladies to look like real flesh and blood, and even patrician flesh and blood. She shows them how to group themselves, how to fall into natural attitudes, to sit or stand, to take up one of the showy volumes on a table and seem really to examine its illustrations, to exchange little friendly greetings with one another, and, above all, not to abandon themselves to vacant contemplation of the audience. In the matter of gloves, shoes, hairdressing, and all small details, Madame Vestris herself could not have been more exacting. 'And mind,' says the arbitrary Myra, 'I will have no lip-salve used in this theatre, making your mouths look as if you were in the last stage of scarlet-fever; and no hairpinning.'

This last mysterious phrase is fully understood by the young ladies to whom it is addressed. It simply means that the use of a smoke-blackened hairpin, by which some fair coryphées intensify the lustre of their eyes, is forbidden at the Frivolity.

The result of this wise tyranny is a happy one. Very fair and fresh are the faces of Mrs. Brandreth's corps de ballet, while many a hard-working young woman learns the elements of good acting from Myra's judicious instructions.

Herman goes home that day with a mind quite at ease. He had dreaded the effect of his marriage upon Myra, weakly and foolishly perhaps, since he was not responsible for any fancies of hers. It is an infinite relief to him to find that she can take matters so easily, and even ask to be presented to his wife.

'It would have been difficult to keep those two apart if I am to go on writing for the Frivolity,' he muses; 'but I don't think now that there's any danger in their meeting. Myra will be sensible enough not to be too confidential with my wife.'

He remembers his conversation with Editha on the rocky margin of the Pennant, and he feels very sure that his young wife would not care to accept among her acquaintance that other who jilted him years ago. He trusts to Mrs. Brandreth's discretion, however, and would not for worlds warn her against any revelation of the past.

The first night of *Kismet* comes after three more weeks of laborious preparation, and day and night rehearsals during the last week, and the last two of these full dress, with lights and scenery and properties as on the night of performance. In a word, Mrs. Brandreth rehearses a modern comedy—which pretends to be an intellectual effort—as carefully as a provincial manager of the first-class rehearses his Christmas pantomime.

The plot of the play is simple, but affords large scope for passion. Estella Bond, a girl of humble birth and position, has been engaged to Paul Mortmain, a landscape painter and a young man of family; they have loved with intensity, and have felt themselves intended for each other by fate. The man, by a sudden turn of Fortune's wheel, has all at once become possessed of large wealth; whereupon, urged by a worldly counsellor, who shows him that the promised wife of Paul Mortmain, the painter, the nobody, is no fitting mate for Paul Mortmain, master of the great Mortmain estates, he deserts his betrothed, first executing a deed of gift which is to give her independence.

Her first use of independence is to educate herself to the level of her false lover; her second, to transfer the twenty thousand pounds he has bestowed upon her to the Asylum for Superannuated Governesses.

'I have education now,' she says, 'and can fight the battle of life!'

She seeks an engagement as governess or companion; obtains one in the latter capacity with Mrs.

Wilding, a young widow residing at Nice; arrives at the widow's villa, and finds that the widow is seriously disposed to sink that title for wife, the husband in view being Paul Mortmain.

Mrs. Wilding, lovely, weak, aristocratic, and gushing, confides freely in Estella, who, on her part, contrives to avoid encountering Paul Mortmain, till a happy stage accident brings them face to face at the end of the second act, and evokes from Estella a withering denunciation of the man's meanness, a scathing repudiation of his would-be generosity—his twenty thousand pounds, which have gone ' to solace the declining days of women who have known enough of the worthlessness of men's love and the hollowness of men's oaths to prefer toil, helplessness, solitude, dependence—ay, starvation—to the bitterness of violated faith and wasted affection.'

She pours a flood of angry passion upon her lover's shame-bowed head; every stage of that long speech, broken only by interjectional remonstrances from the lover, rises in intensity, wavers from scorn to tenderness, from anger to love—yet always mounting in passion—till the final words which bid him leave her, and forget that he has ever loved or ever wronged her, as she from that hour will blot his name and image from her mind. Little perhaps in the fabric of the play: only that skilful use of old materials which marks the originality of the nineteenth century; but the language is forcible and eloquent, and the acting has the fire of true genius. That second act stamps the success of *Kismet*.

'I said there was go in it,' remarks Lord Earlswood, contemplating the ruin of his gloves, which he has split in the storm of applause that greeted Myra's recall. 'The fellows in the stalls like to see two women quarrelling about one man. It's agreeable to masculine self-esteem. Haw!'

The third act shows Paul Mortmain's impassioned pursuit of the woman he has wronged. He has been false to his destiny in leaving her. His old fancy about fate has never quite left him. Nothing has gone well with him since his desertion of Estella. His favourite horse has thrown him viciously; he has taken a fever while electioneering in his county town, and has escaped Death's clutch by the skin of his teeth. Wealth has proved something less than happiness. He now humiliates himself before the woman who once loved him; but she tells him love died with the death of respect. He is no more to her than the strangers she passes in the streets. Let him marry the lovely widow who adores him.

'Butterflies are fond of flowers,' replies Paul. 'I would as soon have the butterfly's love as the widow's—their brain-power must be about equal.'

'You have wronged me,' says Estella; 'you shall not wrong her. You have broken your promise to me; you must keep your promise to her. Prudence as well as honour demands it. No man can be twice disloyal with impunity.'

Estella leaves him in the widow's boudoir, which is the scene of this last act. He seats himself at Mrs. Wilding's davenport, and writes his final appeal to his old love, not without a contemptuous allusion to the volatile widow, who has taken his fancy captive for a while, but never touched his heart. This letter, written with passionate haste, is blotted in Mrs. Wilding's blotting-book. She enters immediately upon Paul's exit, sees the disturbed state of the davenport, the papers thrown about, the pens ruthlessly scattered, and is attracted by the thick black impression on the blotter. 'Paul's hand!'

She is curious enough to tear out the sheet of blotting-paper and hold it up to the light, and there reads disjointed sentences of Paul's letter.

He returns just as she has locked the evidence of his perfidy in the secret drawer of the davenport, returns with a letter in his hand, his own, sent back unopened by Estella, who is on the point of leaving for England.

In his anger with his first love he returns to his second. He throws himself at Laura's feet, tells her that in her innocent and gentle nature he has found the balm for an old wound that has pierced deep, but is not incurable—offers her that milk-and-waterish affection which men who have squandered all their wealth of emotion upon the idol of their youth generously bestow on the consoler of their riper years; but offers it with such fever and energy as might pass current for genuine passion.

Laura fools him to the top of his bent, hears all he has to say, and then shows him the blotting-paper.

Satisfied with his humiliation, she is generous and womanly enough to help him.

'Estella loves you,' she says; 'I guessed her secret the day you met—read it in her face. My suspicions had been awakened by her studious avoidance of you, and I brought about that unexpected meeting in order to test you both. I saw enough in those few moments of surprise and agitation to convince me that I had never possessed your heart, that she had never lost it.'

She goes on to suggest that he shall pretend to have received a telegram announcing that the whole of his fortune has been ingulfed in a bank failure. He shall seem to be reduced at a blow to his old position of dependence on a precarious profession, the exercise of which he has abandoned long enough to have lost much of his old skill—all his old patrons.

He puts this plan into execution with some dexterity, aided by the minor characters, whose comedy enlivens the scene; and Estella, haughty, determined to the last, at the moment of starting for the railway-station, hears that her lover is a pauper, and hears him ridiculed and insulted by Mrs. Wilding, who pretends to exult in his downfall.

This undeserved humiliation moves her more than all. In a noble burst of passion she turns upon Laura, denounces her unwomanly conduct, and then flings herself upon Paul's breast, whereat the happy-dispositioned widow breaks into a peal of rippling laughter, and Estella learns that she has been duped.

So the play—with its light-comedy underplot—ends in everybody's happiness, as a stage-play should end, and Mrs. Brandreth achieves one of those signal triumphs which make an actress's renown.

Editha and her husband have watched the play together, seated side by side in the snug little stage-box, and not once has Herman left his wife throughout the performance, anxious as he may have been to slip behind the scenes and hear what the actors think of the success of each act. He has kept his place by Editha, who has looked and listened almost breathlessly, from the first line to the last, with an anxiously-beating heart. It is the first time she has assisted at any triumph of Herman's, and her cheek glows and her eye brightens as she turns to him at the fall of the curtain.

'I am so glad, Herman,' she says, in her low sweet voice. That is all.

'You really like the piece, dear? That's right. The house is tremendously noisy, isn't it? But these first nights are so delusive. There's an electric current of good-nature circulating among the audience. Even the critics applaud heartily, you see, and yet perhaps some of them will go home and abuse the play.'

Lord Earlswood and Mr. Lyndhurst come into the box to congratulate the author and to be presented to the author's wife, and Herman, whether he likes it or not, has to admit Hamilton Lyndhurst to the roll of Editha's acquaintance. A thing hardly to be avoided anyhow, as Lyndhurst is always to the fore in literary and artistic circles, and is made much of by those very people whose society is most agreeable to Herman.

'Dooced well little Walters plays the widow,' says Lord Earlswood; 'the first time she's ever risen above your waiting-maid business. Brandreth taught her every bit of business, every look and tone; almost made a lady of her, in short. It was wonderful to see her train that slangy little beggar. That laugh was Brandreth's. She taught little Walters note by note. Finest thing in drilling I ever saw; they used to go at it for a quarter of an hour at a stretch; I heard 'em one morning.'

'How clever Mrs. Brandreth must be, and how patient!' says Editha warmly. She is grateful to the actress whose art has helped Herman to achieve success.

Hamilton Lyndhurst looks at her curiously. Herman has just slipped out of the box, and gone behind the scenes to congratulate Myra, as in duty bound.

'Yes, Mrs. Brandreth is clever,' assents Lyndhurst, in his tranquil legato tones; 'one of the cleverest women in London, and a woman whose genius is always undergoing development. She'll give the world some startling proof of her cleverness before she has done with it.'

'I think she has given sufficient evidence of her genius by to-night's performance,' replies Editha.

'And what exquisite taste she has shown in every detail! Herman has reason to be grateful to her.'

'And no doubt is—eminently grateful; authors always are,' says Lyndhurst. 'There's hardly a manager in London whose dinner-table is not resplendent with the tributary *epergnes* and claret-jugs of grateful dramatists.'

'Nice taste in colour, hasn't she?' asks Earlswood, still singing Myra's praises. 'Nothing in the draperies or dresses to set one's teeth on edge.'

'Pearly grays, changeful opals, amaranth, and primrose—gentle reposeful tints that remind one of Leighton's pictures,' says Lyndhurst.

'How do you like the moral of your husband's play, Mrs. Westray?' asks Lord Earlswood. 'It has a moral, I suppose?'

'"There is no moral, little or big, in the *Iliad*,"' says Lyndhurst, quoting De Quincey. 'The greatest works of literary art have been innocent of moral teaching. Mr. Westray's play inculcates no moral, but it illustrates a universal truth. A man can love honestly but once in his life; all after feeling is mere imitation of the first and only genuine passion.

The French mind has a knack of telling the secrets of humanity in a touch-and-go proverb: *On revient toujours à ses premiers amours.*'

A look of distress clouds Editha's face for a moment.

'I don't think my husband would agree with you upon that question, Mr. Lyndhurst,' she answers gravely.

'And yet he has written *Kismet*, which deifies first love, and degrades a second attachment to mere fancy and foolishness,' says Lyndhurst lightly. 'I leave you to examine him as to his intentions, Mrs. Westray, and arrive at his real meaning if you can.'

Editha listens with a disquieted heart. Has not Herman confessed, with praiseworthy frankness, that his first love has not been given to her? And here in this stage-play of his own writing—and it may be that a man unconsciously and involuntarily reveals his convictions through his art—Herman has shown her that first love is a thing imperishable, immortal as the soul which it illumines with its divine fire.

'Could I ever love any one else as I love him?'

she asks herself. 'If we were parted to-morrow, and I were to live half a century, would his image ever be faded, or his influence upon my life be lessened? True love is above time or change.'

She remembers that her lover has described that first attachment of his as something less than pure love. Here is a loophole for hope.

Lord Earlswood retires presently, and follows Herman to the greenroom. Hamilton Lyndhurst remains until Herman's return. He has a knack of making himself agreeable to women of every rank, from a dowager duchess of seventy to a *lionne* of the Château des Fleurs or Jardin Mabille, and he contrives to make his conversation pleasing to Editha in this quarter of an hour *tête-à-tête*. He shows her the notabilities among the audience, an attention which Herman's natural anxiety for the success of his play has prevented his paying his wife. Mr. Lyndhurst knows everybody, and can say something amusing about everybody—not always the most good-natured thing that can be said of a fellow human creature, but always said with an easy good-natured air, which takes the sting out of sarcasm.

Editha listens with a certain interest, yet with some degree of constraint. Mr. Lyndhurst belongs to that new world to which her husband has admitted her; a world in which all man's loftiest feelings and moral qualities seem absolutely at a discount; a world in which to be clever and get the better of one's neighbour appears the one positive virtue; a world in which every man and woman exists for his or her own exclusive benefit, and bends every faculty to one relentless pursuit, individual advantage; a world in which every traveller glides along a single line of rail to his own particular terminus, and regards the comfort and well-being of all other wayfarers as a question remote from the purpose of his being, a subject upon which philanthropists may squander their superfluous energies, and by means of which loud-mouthed agitators may bring themselves into notice.

Herman comes back to the box looking radiant. The actors are delighted with the piece, and pronounce it a greater success than *Hemlock*.

'You shall have your victoria next week, darling,' he whispers to Editha.

Carriage or no carriage is a question that has been discussed between Mr. and Mrs. Westray more than once during the last three weeks. Herman does not like to see his wife deprived of a luxury to which she has been accustomed. Editha pleads on the side of prudence. She is anxious to be a prudent economical wife, and she feels that existence in the Fulham villa is more expensive than it ought to be, and that her notions of housekeeping, as illustrated in her dealings with Jane the cook, are somewhat weak and shadowy.

Herman is in such good humour with all the world that he forgets his old idea of Mr. Lyndhurst as an acquaintance to be dropped after his marriage, and invites that gentleman to dinner.

'Come to us to-morrow, if you've nothing better to do,' he says; 'I've asked Mrs. Brandreth. She is dying to know you, Editha. To-morrow will suit you, I suppose, won't it, dear?'

'To-morrow is Sunday, you know, Herman.'

'Of course. Sunday is the only day she can come to us. I hope your cook will manage to give us an eatable dinner; or perhaps it would be better to go to the Star and Garter. It would be a pleasant drive down to Richmond, wouldn't it, Lyndhurst?'

'The Star and Garter by all means, rather than inflict trouble upon Mrs. Westray,' replies Lyndhurst. 'Let the dinner be my affair as well as yours, Westray; and we may as well ask some more people. Little Miss Walters, for instance — a most amusing beg — a very estimable young lady, Mrs. Westray — and Earlswood. He'll be awfully savage at being shut out if Brandreth comes.'

'I asked Earlswood just now. He comes in any case.'

Editha turns to her husband with that serious look of hers which impressed him at their first meeting—that expression which he then called strong-mindedness.

'I shall be very happy to receive your friends in our own house, Herman, even on Sunday,' she says; 'but I certainly would not go to an hotel to dine upon a Sunday evening.'

'Don't you think that's a distinction without a difference, Mrs. Westray?' asks Lyndhurst. 'You are fond of social straw-splitting in the country. However, I, for my part, shall esteem it a greater honour to dine with you in your own house than anywhere else.'

'So be it. Seven o'clock to-morrow then, Lyndhurst. You know Bridge-end House?'

'Perfectly.'

'We're almost neighbours of yours, by the way.'

'Within a stone's throw.'

Mr. Lyndhurst accompanies Mrs. Westray to her carriage, and watches it depart.

'She reminds me of Clarissa Harlowe,' he says to himself, as he stands waiting for his brougham, 'and is at least a century behind the age she lives in. But she is just the one fresh, fair, unspotted, and perfect woman it has been my lot to meet. For such a woman as that I would turn virtuous, and eschew cakes and ale.'

'I wish we could avoid Sunday dinner-parties, Herman,' Editha says gently, as they drive away from the theatre.

'We can't, dear, while we live in civilised society.'

The honeymoon is over, and the husband answers with marital authority.

'We'll go to Long-acre on Monday, darling, and choose your carriage,' he says gaily, putting his arm round his wife's waist.

'Dear Herman, it is so good of you to think about it; but I can do very well without a carriage. And unless you are quite sure you can afford it—'

'I can afford it easily. The success of *Kismet* will put hundreds in my pocket; and instead of walking about the dull old Fulham lanes, you shall drive in Hyde Park, or to Richmond or Wimbledon.'

'What is the moral of *Kismet*, Herman?' Editha asks irrelevantly.

'Moral, my dear! I don't think there is a moral.'

'Yet it seems to mean, Herman, if it means anything, that a man can love only once. Paul thinks he is cured of his first love, but the end shows that first love is destiny.'

'Of course. When it is real love, like mine for you.'

'But I am not your first love, Herman. You have confessed as much.'

'I have confessed that you are not the first woman who ever seemed charming in my sight; not the first woman I ever made love to. But you are the first I have ever deeply and really loved.'

'Are you sure of that, dearest?'

'Very sure. As sure as I am that we can afford a victoria, and that the wretched female who calls herself a cook will spoil the dinner to-morrow.'

CHAPTER VII.

'The happiness of life is made up of minute fractions—the little, soon forgotten charities of a kiss, a smile, a kind look, a heartfelt compliment in the disguise of playful raillery, and the countless other infinitesimals of pleasurable thought and genial feeling.'

HERMAN's prophecy about the dinner is not unrealised. Jane the cook has not been dismissed abruptly, as he desired. She is a young person of eminently respectable appearance, who seems good-natured, and anxious to please. She has wept at any allusion to warning, and appealed to Editha's soft-heartedness. She has declared piteously that no former master ever complained of her cooking, and she has thrown the burden of all her shortcomings upon that mute offender, the kitchen-range. No one—not a professed cook at seventy guineas a year—could send up a decent dinner from such a range. It is a range of demoniac inconsistency, and will roast the joint to a cinder and leave the poultry half raw. It will send up stony-hearted potatoes and reduce cauliflowers to a watery pulp. It will dry macaroni to chips, yet hardly afford heat enough to penetrate a pair of soles.

Jane declares with tears that the range is preying upon her mind, and that she can't sleep for thinking of it. The parlour-maid, who happens to be Jane's first cousin, sustains her relation's statement. 'Them open ranges ain't a bit of use, mum,' she says. 'You scarcely see 'em anywhere's now, since the kitchingers have come up.' So Editha informs her husband that she fears they will never get on without a new kitchen-stove, though with inward wonder how the great open fire at Lochwithian had contrived to cook everything so nicely, with aid from the charcoal hot-plate only on state occasions; and Herman, ever careless about household trifles, calls at Molding and Korness's *en passant*, and tells them to send him in the best thing in kitcheners. The article is out of their line, perhaps, but they can order it from the proper people.

The kitchener being set, with a good deal of dirt, muddle, and general upheaving of the kitchen department, proves itself curiously imitative of the superseded range. The potatoes still exhibit a tendency to stony-heartedness; the cauliflowers are still pulpy; the soles make up in grease what they want in cooking.

Editha gently suggests that the looked-for improvement has not yet shown itself.

Jane has recourse to the corner of her white apron—a very clean girl, Jane, in the matter of aprons—and protests that no master ever was so hard to please as Mr. Westray.

'But really, Jane, the fish was underdone. I tried to eat it myself, but couldn't.'

'You see, mum, a new kitchener never works quite right; when I get to know my stove it will be different. Leastways, if master has got the right kind of stove. I can't say as I quite hold with this one.'

Happily for Mr. and Mrs. Westray, their guests upon this particular Sunday evening are not people who care very much whether their dinner be good, bad, or indifferent. Lord Earlswood is entirely without gastronomical taste or refinement; Hamilton Lyndhurst is learned in the nicest shades of high-art cookery, but is able, when he finds himself face to face with a badly-cooked dinner, to suspend his appetite in a manner, satisfy the mere cravings of nature with the wing of a fowl and his dinner-roll, and put off the actual process of dining till tomorrow; Mrs. Brandreth is too *spirituelle* to care for the pleasures of the table; and Barkly Tollemy, the dramatic critic, who completes the small party, is an intellectual giant, who takes whatever is set before him in the way of meat or drink with a serenity which is the distinguishing characteristic of himself and his writing.

Myra has never been more charming than on this occasion. There is a repose in her manner which is different from the received idea of a comedy-actress. She wears black velvet, high to the throat, with ruffles of old guipure. A pearl pendent, and a single pearl in each small ear, are her only ornaments. In this dress her graceful figure and aristocratic head appear to perfection, and Editha thinks her handsomer in this softly-lighted room than last night in the glare of the footlights.

The two women get on pretty well together on

this first meeting, though they have few thoughts in common. Editha thanks the actress for her exquisite impersonation of Herman's heroine, and they talk a good deal of his dramatic works, past, present, and to come. But of the past—of those youthful days when she and Herman were playfellows, neighbours, friends, and ultimately lovers—Myra says not one word. Time enough to speak of that unforgotten past when the hour for such revelation ripens. To-night Mrs. Brandreth obtains credit for tact and kindly feeling by this wise reticence. Any allusion to his early manhood would have been painful to Herman, and he is grateful to Myra for her discretion.

Mrs. Brandreth contemplates the small household with an eye that notes every detail. The ill-cooked dinner, the slow service which lengthens its humiliation, gratify her angry soul; for she sees Herman's irritation, and knows that such petty vexations are sometimes strong enough to weaken the bonds of love. She sees Editha's woe-stricken look when the turkey poult crumbles off his bones under the carving-knife, as if he had been discovered at some banquet-table at

Pompeii, and lapsed into dust at exposure to the upper air. She notes the many small annoyances which vex the husband, the secret anxieties of the wife, and tells herself that life's honeymoon is over.

'Foolish people!' she thinks. 'If they lived at an hotel and dined at a *table-d'hôte*, they might go on being turtle-doves for the next ten years. But servants and an ill-managed house will estrange them more surely than the treachery of false friends.'

Dinner once done with, its manes appeased with a glass of maraschino or chartreuse, and a bottle of burgundy circulating among the four gentlemen, the evening is pleasant enough. Mr. Tollemy is in good form, and talks metaphysics in a manner which delights Herman and sorely puzzles Editha. Where, in that region of abstract thought to which Mr. Tollemy soars after his second glass of chambertin, is there a place for the simple creed which has made life—and the dim world beyond life—so sweet to her thoughts, so easy of comprehension, so straight and clear and good? That Mr. Tollemy talks well, and that Herman and he understand each other, she knows; but when she tries to follow them, she feels like one lost in some shadowy wood, where unclean things lurk among the undergrowth, and may start out upon her at any moment.

Lyndhurst tries to interest her, but fails. She is listening to Herman. In her abstraction she forgets that it is time for her to rise, until, looking across at Mrs. Brandreth, she sees a shade of weariness on that lady's face, Lord Earlswood's conversation not being particularly interesting, and is reminded of her duties as hostess.

The two ladies retire to the drawing-room, where numerous wax-candles twinkle gaily in crystal sconces against the walls, and where there is abundance of old china, photographs, and flowers to admire, Herman being in the habit of bringing home pretty things, and not being thoughtful enough in financial matters to consider that these perpetual droppings of stray sovereigns and five-pound notes will wear away the most substantial income.

Again the talk is of Herman and dramatic art. The open piano suggests music, and Editha plays a sacred air of Mendelssohn's with perfect feeling. Mrs. Brandreth declines when asked to play or sing.

'I know no sacred music,' she says. 'I fear you would be shocked if I were to sing a French ballad or a German student's song, and those are the only airs I have at my fingers' ends.'

Editha does not say she would not be shocked, so the subject drops, until the gentlemen appear, when Lord Earlswood pleads warmly for Chaumont's famous ballad, 'La première Feuille,' and, Herman entreating also, Mrs. Brandreth apologises to Editha, and sings deliciously that most bewitching of *chansons*.

The gentlemen implore her not to leave the piano till she has sung something else, and she obeys with a pretty deprecating air, and sings a fine patriotic song, to be found in books of Volkslieder, 'Des Deutschen Vaterland.' She sings it with a dash and spirit that delight her auditors. Mr. Tollemy's gray head waggles enthusiastically over the piano, and the four gentlemen join in the chorus :

'O nein, O nein, O nein!
Sein Vaterland muss grösser sein!'

When Myra has risen from the piano, Hamilton Lyndhurst seats himself unasked, strikes a few chords, and sings a little love song of Shelley's in the noblest baritone voice that Editha has ever heard. Song is Mr. Lyndhurst's one gift, and he possesses that gift in a superlative degree. Few professional singers of the day who would not fear such a rival. While the deep rich voice dwells on the sweet sad words, with perfect enunciation of every syllable, Editha forgets that it is Sunday evening, and that Shelley is a bard who would hardly find a place among *Hymns Ancient and Modern*.

Lyndhurst looks up at the fair grave face, and sees that rapt look, which bespeaks a listener with a soul for melody.

'Come,' he says, 'I'll sing something better than Shelley for you, Mrs. Westray.'

He sings 'Rock of Ages,' as that sublime hymn has been rarely sung in a drawing-room; sings as with religious fervour; sings with a simple intensity of feeling that brings a flood of tears to Editha's eyes. He sees her turn away and hide her face in her handkerchief, and smiles gravely to himself as he bends over the piano, playing the closing chords softly, slowly, with a dying fall. And not a note more will he sing to-night, though Myra entreats for a song of Blumenthal's.

'There's comfort still, she is assailable,' he says to himself.

It is after midnight when the guests depart, and when Herman comes back to the drawing-room he finds Editha standing by the piano with a thoughtful face.

'Herman,' she begins, with ever so slight a tremulousness of tone, 'I must ask you not to give any more Sunday dinner-parties. I always went to evening service at Lochwithian, and I should like to do the same here. Will you mind very much if we dine at six o'clock on Sundays, and invite our friends on any other day than Sunday?'

Herman shrugs his shoulders. He sees that his wife is very much in earnest. That strong-mindedness he dreaded has come out already. He remembers what Dewrance said about their unfitness for each other, and has an uncomfortable feeling that they are on the threshold of their first quarrel.

'My dear love,' he says, 'to deprive me of the right to invite my friends on Sunday is to sever me from some of my pleasantest associations. There is Tollemy, for instance, one of the cleverest men I know, and a most valuable ally. You'll see how *Kismet* will be reviewed in the *Day Star* to-morrow. Now Sunday is Tollemy's great day for dining with his friends. He prefers the *sans gêne* of his club on week-days.'

'And are we to profane the Sabbath, Herman, because Mr. Tollemy likes dining out on that day, and will praise your play in the *Day Star?* Isn't that buying his good word at the price of principle?'

'I was not brought up in Glasgow, and have no Sabbatarian leanings,' answers Herman, pale with anger. 'As for influencing Tollemy, you don't know what you are talking about. He is a man whose society is only too much in request, and who does me honour when he consents to eat an ill-cooked dinner in my house. By the way, that woman must go to-morrow, Editha, if you wish me to dine at home.'

'If I wish you to dine at home! Herman, how can you say that? It is not very much that I ask —only that we may have no more Sunday dinner-parties. When I thought of the peaceful Sunday evenings at Lochwithian, the quiet little church, the simple earnest congregation, Mr. Petherick's kind voice and thoughtful teaching, full of faith and hope, and all that is brightest in religion, and heard you and Mr. Tollemy talking of that last book which has tried to argue Christianity into a fable, I felt as if I had fallen from a happy God-fearing world into the company of sceptics and infidels.'

'My dear Editha, if you would think more of the dinner and less of the after-dinner conversation, you would be a better wife for a literary man who has his way to make in the world,' replies Herman, stifling a yawn as he lights his chamber candle. 'I wonder what the *Day Star* will say of *Kismet?*'

CHAPTER VIII.

'Felicity, pure and unalloyed Felicity, is not a plant of earthly growth; her gardens are the Skies.'

THAT first difference of opinion—it can hardly be called a quarrel—ends as such disputes usually do between newly-wedded lovers. Each surrenders a little. Herman promises only to invite people on Sunday when hard pushed by circumstances. Editha promises to find a better cook, but stands like a rock to attendance at Sunday-evening service at the grave old parish church. Jane Tubbs departs, tearful and reproachful to the last, casting the burden of her sins on the kitchener; and Ann Files comes in her stead, after a charwoman, suggested by the housemaid, has come into clean the numerous corners, cupboards, and secret places in which Miss Tubbs has accumulated all the dirt and broken crockery that has accrued during her reign. Three out of six of the Etruscan beer-jugs are carried off in the dustcart with other fragmentary delf; and on the first morning of her service the new cook informs Editha that there isn't a pie-dish or a pudding-basin in the place, that the bread-pan is cracked, and that that there isn't a dish belonging to the kitchen dinner-service that doesn't leak, 'along of letting 'em stand too long in the oven,' explains cook.

Cook number two is stout and middle-aged, a matron of eminently respectable appearance. She is a considerable improvement upon the last functionary in culinary skill, and contrives to send up savoury little dinners which do not offend Herman's educated senses. This is an unspeakable relief to Editha, who has grown to regard dinner-time as the baneful hour of every day. She has yet to discover that this treasure of culinary art has a hungry family circle residing in an adjacent lane, and deriving their chief sustenance from Mr. Westray's kitchen. Jane Tubbs contented herself with wholesale wastefulness and the liberal entertainment of an extensive circle of acquaintance; Ann Files robs more systematically, introduces a more orderly system of expenditure, and therefore appears more honest. Those differences in the weekly bills which have perplexed Editha no longer occur; but the bills are uniformly heavy.

'We seem to eat a great deal of bread, Files,' Editha remarks, blushing.

'Yes, mum; both the young women are hearty eaters, and I know you wouldn't like me to stint them in *bread*,' replies Files.

'Of course not. I should be sorry for them to be stinted in anything.'

'To be sure, mum. Any lady would,' rejoins the cook, with dignity, as one who has a nice perception of what a lady's feelings ought to be. 'As for me, if the baker never comed it wouldn't make much difference; half a slice at breakfast is all I trouble the loaf for.'

This is not unveracious, Mrs. Files preferring malt to wheat, and taking her nourishment from the beer-barrel rather than the bread-pan.

That housekeeping is a very expensive business, Editha has not been slow to discover. She pays her bills weekly, and is precise and careful in the inspection of the tradesmen's books, yet somehow everything seems to cost a great deal more than it ought. There is never anything left from the late dinner that can be made available for the kitchen next day. Joints resolve themselves into 'pickings' for those voracious housemaids' supper; a hash is not to be thought of; curry the housemaids cannot eat; 'and I shouldn't like to put a curry made of twice-cooked meat before master, mum,' says Files, conscientiously; 'it would seem like imposing upon him.'

A beefsteak-pudding for the early dinner swallows four pounds of steak. The loins of pork that Editha has paid for under the régime of Jane Tubbs would have kept an eating-house going. Ann Files affects nice little bits of corned beef, which never appear as less than nine shillings in the butcher's book, and are never to be heard of next day. Groceries of all kinds disappear in the same proportions, and there is a heavy demand for eggs, butter, cheese, and bacon. Candles are lively, and flour is never dull. Editha, without exactly supposing that she is being robbed, has an uneasy sense that the housekeeping expenses are much heavier than they ought to be.

She has to ask Herman so often for money; and the sums he gives her—always liberal—seem to melt through her fingers. She wonders how her father can have contrived to support that great household at Lochwithian, and no longer marvels at those occasional bemoanings on the subject of finance which have rippled the calm current of home-life at the Priory.

Herman is unconsciously a cause of expense. He has a habit of saying, when his dinner does not particularly please him, 'My love, couldn't you give me a wild duck now and then?' or, 'My dear, I saw quails at the Roscius yesterday. Let us have some quails;' and Editha will give any price the poulterer likes to charge for the birds Herman fancies. He likes an omelet for breakfast, and on the strength of these omelets, Ann Files takes in two-shillings-worth of eggs daily.

Herman is now able to invite his friends to dinner without enduring tortures as each dish is placed on the table; but the cost of these little dinners is awful. Ann Files is a disciple of that French artist who could reduce half a dozen hams into an essence to be contained in an ounce bottle. A shin of beef, two knuckles of ham, and one of veal barely suffice for the small tureen of clear soup which begins the banquet. True the clear soup is good, but still better is the noble mess of beef *à la mode* which Ann Files's sister-in-law carries home with her that night, in a spoutless beer jug, under cover of the darkness; and savoury are those nice little shanks of ham which Ann Files's brother discusses at breakfast next morning. The Fulham confectioner's entrées at seven and sixpence and half a guinea are dirt cheap as compared with Ann Files's veal olives—a small dish whereof necessitates the sacrifice of half a fillet of veal—or those mutton cutlets which can only be put on the table at the cost of a whole neck of mutton.

'I uses the scrag and all the orkard bits for my gravies, you see, mum,' explains Files; notwithstanding which the article gravy-beef figures like a running accompaniment to the joints in the butcher's book.

Nothing ever remains over at these banquets, however small the party. It would seem as if Mrs.

Westray's guests reversed the order of things, and adapted their consumption to the supply. But this phenomenon of total evanishment Mrs. Files is able to explain in a simple and rational manner, when interrogated timidly by Editha.

'That young man as comes to wait, mum, and a very respectable well-conducted young man he is; no flirting nor nonsense with the young women; but as for appetites, I never see anything like it. The supper that young man eats, after he's taken in the tea and coffee, would astonish you. And it's customary to give them their suppers off the dishes as leave the table, which I'm sure you wouldn't like me to do less than is usual; besides which, if you balked him that way, he'd be putting his fingers into my dishes, and nibbling of 'em outside the dining-room door.'

'O, the man must have his supper, of course,' says Editha.

'I'm very glad we've no footman, Herman,' she remarks that evening, when she and her husband happened to speak of domestic matters; 'the way that young man Moiser eats is really dreadful.'

'You mean the fellow that waits. He's a very decent waiter, that fellow, moves about quietly, doesn't rattle the spoons or jingle the glasses. Let him eat as much as he likes, dear, and don't you worry yourself about it. By the bye, what a charming little dinner you gave us last night! We are improving in our housekeeping.'

'I'm so glad you think so, Herman,' Editha says, brightening; 'but I'm afraid these little dinners are very expensive.'

'Of course, dear; everything that's worth anything costs money; but they must be much cheaper at home than anywhere else. In the matter of wines, for instance; that moselle we were drinking last night would be fifteen shillings a bottle at Richmond or Greenwich, and it only stands me in seven and sixpence.'

'O Herman, will you send in a little more moselle, please? I put out the last half-dozen bottles yesterday.'

'What, the six cases gone already?'

'Yes, dear; your friends drink so much at dinner. I used to put out three bottles for a small party, but Moiser told me he was obliged quite to stint people, and pretend not to see when they looked at him to have their glasses filled; so now I put out five or six, and there is never any left.'

'I daresay Moiser has a liking for moselle,' answers Herman carelessly. Sitting drowsily by the fire in that snug little study of his, he has just hit upon a happy idea for the third volume of his novel; and a man who has a happy idea cannot be expected to throw his thoughts out of gear for the sake of an odd bottle of wine.

And thus domestic life glides on, pleasantly if ruinously. Are not most of the roads to ruin pleasant? Editha is so happy in seeing Herman pleased with his dinner and satisfied with his breakfast, that she commits herself almost unquestioningly to Ann Files the cook; whereby the family in that adjacent lane rejoice greatly, and sundry visiting acquaintance of Mrs. Files, and of Mary Ann the parlourmaid, and Selina the housemaid, have a good time in Mr. Westray's kitchen.

'If one can't have one's young man to supper once in a way, one might as well live in the

Black Hole at Jamaica,' remarks Selina to Mrs. Files.

'I've always been one to stand by my fambly,' says Mrs. Files, after despatching half a sirloin to her kindred in the lane, 'and when I'm out of place I've always a home to go to, and no call to hurry myself about getting a sitiwation till I can suit myself to my own satisfaction.'

The victoria is chosen, and the prettiest pair of horses the Westminster-road can produce are bought to draw it, after much deliberation and consultation, and several exhibitions of their performances before a select party of friends. Herman thinks he has done rather a clever thing in going to the Westminster-road for his cattle, instead of giving the West-end prices for the same. A victoria will not serve to convey Mrs. Westray to dinner parties or theatres, so a miniature brougham has to be added. Horses, carriages, harness, livery, and those etceteras in the way of dandy brushes, carriage ladder, boot-top paste, leathers, and sponges, which are more alarming to the minds of the uninitiated than the larger items, make a hole in one of Herman's loose thousands; so large a hole, in fact, that very little of that particular thousand remains after all is paid.

As a set-off for this vanished thousand he has the satisfaction of seeing his wife in a properly-appointed carriage as befits the wife of a popular writer; and Editha has the delight of calling for her husband at his club three or four times a week, and driving round the Park with him on their way home. Hyde Park has a flattish dullish look to this daughter of mountain and flood, but to drive with Herman is not the less Elysium. The heart creates its own landscape, and true love can be happy in a garret, or within the gray walls of a debtors' prison.

So the days go on—drear November—chill December—Christmas at Lochwithian, where there is gladness and love inexhaustible for the young wife — frosty January — biting February — blusterous March—sweet vernal April. The trees bourgeon and blossom in gardens and Park, the labourer leaves his fireside, the keels of the pleasure boats glide down the bright blue river, and one can fancy that the nymphs and graces dance lightly in the violet-perfumed woodland under the clear spring moon. Herman and Editha have been wedded more than six months, and feel quite old married people. Indeed, to judge by the amount of crockery that has been broken, and the way the edges of the table-knives are knotched and turned, they might have been married six years.

Not yet has Ruth come to visit her married sister, anxious as Editha is for that happiness. The winter has been somewhat severe, and has tried Miss Morcombe sorely. She is not so strong this year as she was last, and Dr. Price advises against any extra exertion just at present. In the summer, perhaps, she may be equal to the journey from Lochwithian to London.

The Squire runs up to town in April, and spends a week with his daughter and son-in-law, and highly approves of their snug little establishment.

'Hope you're not going too fast, Westray,' he remarks sagely. 'Mustn't look upon your literary earnings as certain income, you know. Fashions change—new lights appear. That's how Goldsmith and Sheridan and Scott, and such fellows, always contrived to outrun the constable.'

'If Sheridan's wife had been as prudent as Editha, he would never have come to grief,' replies Herman. 'She won't even order a gown from a French dressmaker, for fear she should ruin me.'

More than once Editha has suggested that Herman's sisters ought to be invited to the villa.

'It would be a pleasant change for them, dear, I should think,' she says.

'Perhaps it might, love; but it wouldn't be a pleasant change for me,' returns Herman frankly. 'The fact is, I've outgrown my sisters. They were always older than I, and the progress of years has aged them more than it has aged me; so that the gulf between us widens. In plain words, they have grown a trifle priggish; take me to task about my books; wish that there was a higher purpose underlying my stories; tell me what Mr. Symcoks, the curate, thinks upon the subject of my latest fiction; regret that I should waste my mental powers upon the composition of worthless evanescent plays; and make themselves altogether disagreeable. No, love, we are too happy in our union to admit any jarring element. We'll send the poor old girls as many presents as you like—music, books, hair-pads, ribbons, silk gowns—but we'll maintain an equable two hundred miles between them and ourselves.'

'Isn't that unkind, Herman?'

'I daresay it is, dear, but it's wise. The goddess of wisdom never was remarkable for her amiability; but she knew a thing or two. Devonshire is the place for my aged sisters. I'd as soon invite the three old ladies with the sewing machinery—I mean to say the spindle and shears institution—as those amiable spinsters.'

The cheerful and congratulatory period of the new year has brought in Messrs. Molding and Korness's account for the furnishing of the domestic nest; an account which in bulk and neatness of caligraphy looks like a lawyer's brief, and the sum-total of which takes Herman's breath for a moment or so, like a header into a December flood. He had no idea that taste was so expensive an item in upholstery. That artistic simplicity, that classic chastity which distinguish Bridge-end House are as costly as any splendour of gilding and crimson brocade which a retired citizen could have chosen for the adornment of his brand-new mansion at Canonbury or Hoxton. Every one of those small devices, which seemed to Herman so clever and inexpensive, figures in Messrs. M. and K.'s account as an important item. Not an inch of ebonised beading, not a bracket or a curtain-loop, but is separately entered.

Herman puzzles over the pages of that account as if it were an essay of Herder's, but he cannot question the precision and honesty of a bill which so rigidly sets out its smallest item, so carefully describes and identifies every object charged for.

He folds up the document with a sigh. The payment of Messrs. Molding and Korness will make a clean sweep of that little capital of which the successful author boasted to Squire Morcombe when he asked for Editha's hand. It will leave Herman shoulder to shoulder with Fortune once again, instead of being a few thousands in advance of necessity. He has been prospering since his marriage. *Kismet* has brought him a great deal of money in a very short time; his novel has been eminently successful, and he is well on with another comedy and another fiction. Henceforth he will be able to afford himself briefest repose from his labours, for, in the words of the greatest of English philosophers, he has given hostages to Fortune. Yet he sees in the wife he loves no 'impediment to great enterprises,' as Lord Bacon calls this tender tie, but rather an incentive to ambition. Before summer has faded from the land he hopes to be a father; sacred name, which thrills him with a strange sweet pride and gladness; holiest of all names given to man, since it is the name man gives his God.

Happy beyond all measure is that spring-time of their wedded life, despite the dissipation of Herman's little capital and the necessity for unremitting work. The young husband devotes all his leisure to his wife. He buys a boat, and keeps it up the river at Teddington, whither they can drive on balmy April afternoons, dine at a little waterside inn, and row up to Hampton or Halliford after dinner, driving home late in the moonlight. Editha is never so happy as when they are quite alone together; and as the spring ripens to summer, the little dinners, at which Mr. Tollemy and other literary lights are entertained, cease for the most part, and Herman and his wife spend their evenings in the garden, he smoking and dreaming, with an occasional lapse into conversation, she reading to him sometimes—she reads beautifully, and it is one of her delights to administer to his pleasure in this way—or working with dextrous fingers at miniature garments of cambric or lawn, which look as if they were intended for that fairy page about whose small person Titania and Oberon quarrelled.

The young wife, worshipping her husband as only a single-minded unselfish woman can worship the imperfect clay to which destiny has mated her, has yet contrived to hold firmly by certain simple rules of her maiden life. She attends all those services of her church which she has been wont to attend, and not even Herman's convenience or inclination, paramount over all lesser things, is allowed to interfere with her performance of this duty. She contrives to do some good in her immediate neighbourhood—visits the dirty cottages in the dirty lanes; sends small gifts of broths and groceries to the sick and aged; strengthens the feeble knees with help material and spiritual; and earns the gratitude of the vicar of her district, whose highest pride it is to call himself a parish priest, and who is never weary of labouring for the welfare of his flock. And these suburban parishes are not easy to manage. They have all the vices of town, and all the ignorance of the country. There are old men and women in those lanes who have never been to London—marvellous as the fact may appear that people can remain supine and incurious with the mightest metropolis in the world at their elbow—yet the vices of London have come down to them: the artifice, the shiftiness, the plausibleness, the intemperance and greed of the metropolitan pauper, are to be found among these incurious Fulhamites, who, having 'never had no call to go to London,' have not troubled themselves to make the journey.

Dewrance dines now and then with Mr. and Mrs. Westray, and is surprised and honestly glad to see them so happy.

Summer comes, and in the late summer the fruition of Herman's hopes. A baby son is put into his inexperienced arms in the dim dawn of an August morning, after a night of watchfulness and anxiety; and he feels that he is verily pledged to the inscrutable goddess Fortune, and that his hand had need be busy and his brain prolific, for the sake of wife and child.

In reality, the wife and child would be but a light burden upon his industry, if he had not cook and housemaids, nursemaid, coachman and horses, wear and tear of stable utensils, breakage of pudding-basins and other kitchen sundries, grease-pot, servants' relations and followers, to provide for as well.

CHAPTER IX.

'Side by side thus we whisper: "Who loves, loves for ever,"
As wave upon wave to the sea runs the river,
And the oar on the smoothness drops noiseless and steady,
 Till we start with a sigh,
 Was it she—was it I—
Who first turn'd to look back on the way we had made?
Who first saw the soft tints of the garden-land fade?
Who first sigh'd, " See, the rose-hue is fading already"?'

EIGHT months more of Herman Westray's wedded life have come and gone since that August morning. The London season is at its height; the Frivolity is crowded nightly; Mrs. Brandreth is more popular than ever, delighting the town in a comedy which is not Herman's. His last effort, produced in the late autumn after his son's birth, has been that gentle failure which kindly critics call a *succès d'estime*. One of his rivals has followed with a clever adaptation from the German—domestic, tender, simple, almost arcadian—and the pretty fancy has taken the town, much to Herman's disgust.

The *chefs-d'œuvre* which secure success for our rivals seem to us such flimsy things. We could have done them ourselves easily, if the central idea had but happened to strike us.

Piqued and disappointed at this humiliating turn in affairs, he is working savagely at a new play, in the progress of which Myra is warmly interested; so much so, that he spends most of his leisure afternoons just now in the elegant little drawing-room of one of the small old houses in Kensington Gore, to which Mrs. Brandreth has removed from sober Bloomsbury. The success of the Frivolity, now firmly established as a popular and fashionable theatre, amply justifies some expansion in the lessee's surroundings; and Mrs. Brandreth's victoria is the prettiest to be seen in the Park; and Mrs. Brandreth's small Sunday dinners are as perfect in their simple unpretentious fashion as dinners can be. She does not astonish her guests with peaches before stawberries have fairly come in; but her wines are exquisite, her *menu* has always some touch of novelty, and she never fatigues her friends by too elaborate a banquet.

Her house is altogether one of the pleasantest in London. She knows only clever people, and eschews the Philistine element. The mercantile and ponderous classes are unrepresented at that cosey round table, where art and literature meet in the freedom of a friendly Bohemianism, which never degenerates into vulgarity or recklessness of speech. Mrs. Brandreth is about the last woman whom any man possessed of the least *savoir faire* would be likely to offend by lack of due reverence for her sex. The very fact that she stands quite alone in the world, and is known to have been superior to any temptations which Lord Earlswood's wealth could offer, gives her an additional claim upon the respect of her circle. She is not fast, or loud, or insolent. There is an easy grace about her manner, with a touch of languor when she is not warmly interested in the topic of the moment—a languor which some people mistake for pride.

She has altered her mode of life considerably since Herman's marriage; it may be her steadily increasing success, or it may be some change in her own nature. She is fonder of society than of old, reads less, is less alone. She takes more pains to cultivate acquaintance likely to assist her professional advancement; goes more into the world; seizes and occupies a more important position in society; works her hardest to be *grande dame* as well as popular actress.

Herman sees the difference, and wonders at it, almost with envy. He has spent his small fortune, and has not found it possible yet awhile to replace those few thousands which melted so easily in his first year of wedded bliss. Myra is growing rich. She has invested her surplus judiciously, under the direction of Hamilton Lyndhurst, who guarantees a safe six per cent upon all such investments. It seems to Herman that in the race of life his old playfellow in getting ahead of him. Her fame is perhaps greater than his, although a trifle less enduring; for however worthless the next generation may account his books, the books will exist in some form, if only to be despised, and afford some record of himself; while the actress's renown can be no more than a tradition.

For Editha this second year of wedded life is

not quite so happy as the first. True that she has her boy for the tender care and delight of her days, —a dawning intelligence which expresses itself as yet only in half-articulate babblings or monosyllabic utterances, which the young mother puzzles out as earnestly as if they were fragments of an inscription on the crumbling wall of a temple dug out of the banks of the Euphrates. To amuse him in his waking hours, to watch him when he sleeps, to nurse him in his small ailments, to take him for airings in the victoria, form the new joys of her existence; but even this happiness cannot make up for the loss of Herman's society, and of him she sees much less this year than last.

The spring is well advanced, and they have had but one boating excursion, and even that one was not unalloyed bliss, for Herman was self-absorbed and inclined to be irritable, taking objection to the east-wind, the cockney oarsmen who menaced the safety of his boat, and the lukewarm condition of the stewed eels at the hotel where they dined.

He works harder than last year, and with less pleasure in his labour. He is nervous and excitable, and there are times when Editha's quiet presence in his study seems to worry and disturb him. Her watchfulness has discovered that he writes less fluently of late; that he throws himself oftener back in his chair to meditate; bites the end of his pen moodily for ten minutes at a time; runs his pen across a page of copy with a vexed impatient air; in a word, finds it difficult to please that most indulgent of all critics, himself.

The flying pen which has been wont to travel over the paper with electric swiftness, driven by thoughts too rapid for mortal hand to keep pace with, now drags along heavily, with only spasmodic spurts now and then to relieve its sluggishness. Editha makes up her mind that Herman is overworked, and tells him so, earnestly imploring him to give himself rest, to pause in the composition of his novel, to postpone the production of his play. The suggestion is to the last degree unwelcome to him. His vanity is quick to take offence.

'You've been influenced by the twaddle in that last review in the *Censor*. I believe they keep those articles standing, and only alter the names of the books and authors, and shift the positions of the paragraphs to make them look fresh. You think I have written myself out?' he says irritably. 'Then I suppose that last chapter I read you seemed flat and dull; had a faded air, eh?'

'Not in the least, Herman; it was lovely; but I am sure you want rest, for all that. You write so much more slowly than you used.'

'Perhaps I write a good deal more carefully.'

'Ah, to be sure; I never thought of that. To my mind you have always written so well that I cannot imagine more care being needed. But I daresay your next novel will be better than anything you have written yet.'

'I hope it may,' says Herman moodily, thinking of his empty coffers, and that some of the Christmas accounts—wine-merchant, corn-merchant, Fortnum and Mason—are still outstanding; and that he has been respectfully solicited more than once to send a cheque. The next stage after respectful solicitation is a lawyer's letter.

That play which progresses so slowly—some alteration or amendment being suggested by Mrs.

Brandreth at each reading—is a thorn in Editha's side. Herman is now rarely at home on Sunday evening. Editha ventures a faint remonstrance one day.

'Our Sunday evenings used to be so happy last year,' she says. 'You went to church with me very often, and we used to have such pleasant walks afterwards up the hill to Wimbledon Common in the starlight.'

'Arcadian and delicious, dear. We'll have just such walks again when my play is finished; but for the moment business is paramount with me. I must make a success at the Frivolity before the season is over. But if you don't like my leaving you, why don't you come to Kensington Gore with me on a Sunday? Mrs. Brandreth is perpetually asking me why you won't come.'

'You know how much I dislike Sunday visiting, Herman.'

'In that case you must not object if we sometimes spend Sunday evening apart.'

'Sometimes, Herman!'

'Sunday is Mrs. Brandreth's only disengaged

evening, you know,' adds Herman, ignoring the somewhat reproachful exclamation.

'Herman, don't you think it is a sin to devote Sunday evening to secular business? It seems to me that no blessing can attend any work which involves the desecration of the Sabbath.'

'My dearest, we don't look at things from quite the same point of view.'

'Indeed, Herman! I fancied we both thought alike upon great subjects, even if we have different ways of acting in matters of detail.'

Long as they have been married, all-confiding as they have been to each other, Herman has contrived to keep his religious opinions very much to himself. Editha has thought him lax, but she has never supposed him an unbeliever in that creed which is to her the very foundation of her life. He knows this, and feels that they are treading upon dangerous ground.

'My dear, the amount of business that I get through at one of Mrs. Brandreth's Sunday evenings is so small that it need scarcely trouble you.'

'And yet you cannot spare me one of those evenings?'

'Well, you see, there is always something. I talk over what I have written with Mrs. Brandreth, and hear her opinion. She has a happy knack of hitting upon good ideas as to situation and stage effect. No outsider can have any idea how the success of a play hinges on these details. Some jokelet which seems utterly inane when one sees it in black and white will set the gallery in a roar, and keep the house in good-humour for a whole evening. And then I meet useful people at her house—critics, newspaper-men, fellows who can give me a lift now and then. You see, as you don't like me to invite them here on a Sunday, it's an advantage for me to meet them at Myra's.'

Editha looks up suddenly, startled by that familiar mention of the actress, and Herman reddens.

'I beg Mrs. Brandreth's pardon for speaking of her by her Christian name,' he says. 'I hear her old friends call her Myra. Curious name, isn't it?' he adds carelessly; 'Myra—not by any means a pretty one.'

'Yes, it is curious,' Editha murmurs thoughtfully.

That utterance of another woman's Christian name has given her quite a shock. Ridiculous, of course, that she should be so weak-minded. She is ashamed of her own folly.

'I hope I have not a jealous nature,' she says to herself, wondering at that sudden pang which shot through her heart for so slight a cause.

But after this she takes a dislike to the Frivolity Theatre and all its associations. She is troubled by Herman's attendance at Mrs. Brandreth's Sunday receptions; he dines in Kensington Gore on many Sundays, and she eats her dinner alone, or countermands the dinner altogether, as a superfluous ceremony, and takes a cup of tea and an egg before going to church. Lenten Sundays these, in every sense. The preacher moralises upon the vanity of human wishes, the brevity of earthly happiness, and she feels that of all the congregation his words come home to her heart most keenly. After church she goes up into her baby's nursery, and sits with him while the nursemaid has her evening out; sits beside the dainty little brazen cot, chintz-curtained and befringed, which Messrs. Molding and Korness have supplied for the heir of all the ages and nothing particular besides; sits reading the *Imitation of Christ* or Jeremy Taylor's *Holy Living*—that wondrous mixture of spiritual truth and shrewdest worldly wisdom; sits for hours reading her good books by the little one's pillow, and only pauses once in a way to wonder how Herman is amusing himself at Kensington Gore.

Could she take a bird's-eye view of Mrs. Brandreth's drawing-rooms, how that gentle heart would be wounded! The front room—by no means large, and a little overcrowded with those various elegant trifles, Sèvres flower-stands, brass-mounted stereoscopes, majolica card-trays supported by chubby Cupids, which enthusiastic admirers have offered as respectful tribute to the popular actress—contains as many people as can find standing room. There is a buzz of conversation, which effectually drowns the classic performance of a German composer at the small marqueterie cottage-piano; but what can people expect if they will play Chopin-and-water with the soft pedal down at a fashionable At Home? The critics are assembled in full force, revelling in the discussion of various late fiascos in literature and art, or according loud and enthusiastic praise to the last delight of the critical mind, some literary weakling, self-conscious as Narcissus, whom the critics adore as an intellectual Hercules.

The inner drawing-room is too small for anything but an oratory or a shrine, and here, in the lowest and most graceful of Louis-Quinze chairs, in a half-reclining attitude, languid, reposeful, picturesque, sits Myra Brandreth, dressed in her favourite black velvet and rose point—the one costume which becomes her to perfection, and which she is too wise to lay aside for the arbitrary varieties of fashion. The square-cut bodice reveals the graceful throat; the century-old lace veils the fair neck, and gives a Madonna-like purity to the dress. Small diamond eardrops and a yellow rosebud fastened in the bosom of her dress are Myra's only ornaments. Her large black fan is painted with pale yellow roses, and dangles from her wrist by a pale yellow ribbon.

'How fond you are of yellow!' says Herman, who alone with the priestess occupies this luxurious sanctuary, half hidden from the occupants of the adjoining room by the deeply-drooping amber curtains, and just large enough to contain a jardinière, a coffee-table, and three easy-chairs.

'Yes, I like the colour; perhaps because it is not a general favourite.'

'The colour of jealousy, of amaranth and asphodel, the chosen flowers of death.'

He is leaning over her chair playing with her fan, furling and unfurling it perpetually for his own amusement. If gentlemen never so amused themselves, fans would be everlasting wear.

'Death and I are very good friends,' replies Myra, with a sigh. 'I have so little to live for.'

'Why, I thought you had everything in the world that can make life worth living—fame, success, money, a profession you adore.'

'Yes, I am very fond of acting. That and music are the only arts which take one out of oneself.'

'In your case I should have fancied self so agreeable a subject that you would hardly care to be carried away from it. I should have supposed you had not a care or a sorrow.'

'Herman!' she exclaims, turning her dark hazel

eyes upon him slowly; they are at their softest tonight, with a veiled look which is almost like tears. 'You ought to know me better than that.'

He remembers another Sunday evening long ago, and a certain question of Myra's, together with the reply he made thereto; remembers with a faint sigh. Would it not have been more generous, would it not have been wiser, to accept what was then offered him? Infinitely wiser than to be hankering after it now, assuredly; but this reply an unobtrusive conscience does not suggest to Mr. Westray.

Would it not have been wiser to have returned to his old love two years ago, to have accepted the gem that was offered to him—not quite a flawless gem, it is true, but with a wonderful sparkle about it? These Sunday evenings at Kensington Gore are so pleasant; Myra's little dinners so much more *recherchés* and various than the little dinners at home, which are apt to repeat themselves. And life is made up of small pleasures; it is an infinite series of nothings. High principles and noble thoughts are like Alpine peaks, very grand and very beautiful to contemplate from a distance; but easy manners and exquisite taste in details are the castors on which the armchair of life runs easily over the carpet of the world.

Myra and Herman talk of old times now and then—talk of the dead-and-gone fathers whom they both loved; and are drawn very near to each other by these tender memories.

'Have you been to Colehaven within the last few years?' Myra asks.

'Not since my mother's death. I used to run down pretty often in her time.'

'I have not been there since my father died and Mrs. Pompion came to fetch me away,' says Myra. 'It is not for want of love, but for want of courage, that I have never been to see my father's grave.'

And then somehow Myra tells the story of her marriage, in her own highly-picturesque representation of which event she appears as the victim of Mrs. Pompion's worldliness—not to say cruelty.

'She made me understand that I was homeless and penniless, and that I should be doing her a wrong by prolonging my dependence upon her an hour longer than I was obliged.'

'You might have found independence with me, Myra,' is the reproachful suggestion.

'Yes, and blighted your career at the very outset,' replies Myra, who remembers perfectly well that at this stage of Herman's life his sole means were represented by a scholarship and 50*l.* a year from his father.

'Poor Charley!' she sighs; 'I never loved him, but he was very good to me.'

Lord Earlswood cuts short these somewhat sentimental conversations now and then by precipitating himself through the curtained archway, and planting himself upon the one available chair. Having very little to say for himself when so planted, he seems slightly in the way. He is painfully jealous of Herman, yet has no ground for complaint, having, in fact, no status. Society in general in the Kensington Gore drawing-rooms is aware of his lordship's jealousy, and of Mrs. Brandreth's sentimental affection for the author; and 'poor Lady Earlswood' and 'poor Mrs. Westray' receive a due amount of somewhat scornful pity.

CHAPTER X.

'Aussi se permit-elle alors de protéger de petits jeunes gens ravissants, des artistes, des gens de lettres nouveau-nés à la gloire, qui niaient les anciens et les modernes, et tâchaient de se faire une grande reputation en faisant peu de chose.'

HERMAN's novel brings him some hundreds, and enables him to pay wine-merchant and corn-merchant and reëstablish his balance at his banker's; but not to save a sixpence. He has acquired extravagant habits, lives among extravagant people, and has that noble recklessness about trifling expenditure which seems the distinguishing characteristic of a superior mind, and which brings so many superior minds to the workhouse. The unheeded pence run away with their big brothers the pounds, and Herman's *menus plaisirs* are almost as costly as Ann Files's hungry relatives. His cigars are the choicest that money can buy, and he has always a liberal supply at the service of his friends. He never touches cards, and boasts of that negative virtue as an example of the prudence which befits a family man; but he spends a good deal of money upon hansom cabs, and a good deal more upon bric-à-brac, indulging his artistic taste to the uttermost when he sees anything worth carrying home to the nest at Fulham. Sometimes he takes Myra a Vienna cup and saucer, rich in costliest gilding, or a Charles Théodore *déjeuner;* for is he not under considerable obligation to that lady for his dramatic successes?

These small gifts are the pabulum of friendship. Does not sage Cecil counsel his son to give many gifts, but small ones, to his patron, if he would be constantly remembered?

The balance at Herman's banker's diminishes with alarming rapidity, and he is just beginning to contemplate a serious reformation in his habits; indeed, on one of those happy evenings when he seems to return to his old self, he goes so far as to announce this virtuous intention to his wife. Never before has he spoken to her of money matters, but has allowed her to suppose that his resources are in a manner inexhaustible.

'I'll tell you what it is, Editha; I mean to turn

over a new leaf,' he says, as she sits opposite to him in the little study by the cheerful evening fire. The April sunset reddens the sky above the flat fields of Fulham, the gray twilight creeps over asparagus-beds and cabbage-gardens, the baby lies in his mother's lap chuckling and crowing at the fire, and lifting up his small mufflered feet to be played with by his admiring parents. Quite a domestic picture, and curiously contrastive to last Sunday evening in Kensington Gore.

'In what way, dearest?' asks the fond wife. 'Not to work so hard, I hope.'

'Quite the contrary, dear. To work harder than ever, and to turn miser. I can't be too careful or too anxious about the future now I've this little one to think about, to say nothing of the procession of brothers and sisters who will naturally follow his footsteps. I shall leave off cigars henceforth.'

'O Herman, you are so fond of your cigar!'

'A pipe is ever so much better.'

'You can't smoke a pipe at your club, dear.'

'Then I shall spend so much the less time at my club.'

'And so much more at home! Ah, Herman, I shall be grateful to your pipe if it brings about that result!'

'And then there's the money I waste in hansom cabs; quite a little fortune for Master Squaretoes here, if it were to accumulate at compound interest. I shall give up cabs and take to walking. Nothing so bad for a man's heart as the perpetual friction of locomotion in which he is only a passive agent.'

Virtuous resolves, so pleasant a subject for conversation by the evening fire, inspired by the companionship of wife and child; but the next time Herman is in a hurry to get to Kensington Gore he hails the smartest hansom on the stand, and gives the man double fare for driving him at the rate of twelve miles an hour.

Early in May the new piece is produced to a brilliant audience, and is a positive success. With this stroke of fortune all Herman's good resolutions melt away. He has but to write to be rich. There is a bottomless gold mine in his ink-pot. He thinks of Sir Walter Scott, who, at nearly sixty years of age, in a brief span of herculean labour, earned by his pen the almost incredible **sum of 100,000l.** ; and he believes that for him, too, literature will be an ever-flourishing pagoda-tree, whose golden fruit he can pluck to the end of his days.

He is intoxicated by the enthusiastic reception of his new play, coming after that odious *succès d'estime*, and his gratitude to Myra for her invaluable **suggestions and her admirable acting is boundless.** He buys a sapphire locket out of the first proceeds of the drama—antique, classical, expensive—and with his own hands hangs it upon Mrs. Brandreth's fair throat. He takes home a snowy-plumed hat for baby the day after, and Editha's eyes fill with tears at the thought that he should have considered the little one.

'And now that the play is produced, dearest, we shall have our old Sunday evenings again, I hope,' Editha says gently.

'Yes, love, I can give you some of my Sundays now. But I am going to put a new comedy on the stocks directly, and I shall want to consult Mrs. Brandreth now and then. She has such a masterly knowledge of dramatic effect.'

'How I envy her the delight of assisting you! It seems as if she were almost a partner in your work.'

'Not quite, dear,' answers Herman, with a supercilious smile; 'but her advice is useful upon all technical points. And then her house is one of the pleasantest I know. One meets such nice people there.'

'If you could only bring the same people here, Herman!' says Editha, with a sigh. She would do anything except sacrifice principle to have her full share in her husband's life, and she feels with a pang that it is slipping away from her somehow. Jealous of Mrs. Brandreth in the vulgar sense of the word she is not, for her mind is too pure to imagine evil. But she envies Myra those gifts which render her society valuable and her house charming to Herman.

'Not so easy, my love. We are farther from town—objection number one. The people who go to Mrs. Brandreth's will drive a mile and a half, but don't care about driving three miles. Then you set your face against Sunday receptions—objection number two. The people I meet at Mrs. Brandreth's like Sunday visiting.'

'Could we not have an evening once a week, on which your friends could come to you in an unceremonious way, Herman?' suggests Editha timidly. 'Dinner-parties are so expensive, and we have quite enough of them already. But perhaps if these people you like so much knew that you were at home on a particular evening, they would come to us.'

'I thought you were too much wrapped up in baby for that kind of thing; we've been degenerating into domesticity since that young gentleman's arrival. However, perhaps it's not a bad idea. I'll get you some cards printed, and we'll have our weekly reception—say Tuesday evening; music and conversation, tea and coffee, light wines, sandwiches. Dr. Johnson says that no man, however intellectual, likes to leave a house exactly in the same condition he entered it. Human nature requires some sustaining element, if only sherry and sandwiches.'

Editha is delighted, for this arrangement will

give her at least one evening in the week on which she will be sure of her husband's society.

Mrs. Westray's Tuesday evenings, in a certain unpretentious way, are a success. Kensington and Chelsea are rich in artists and literary men, and these are Herman's favourite companions. The distance is easy between Fulham and these abodes of art and letters; painters, playwrights, poets, and their natural enemies and boon companions the critics, rattle down to Bridge-end House in hansoms, and walk home in a merry band by moonlight or starlight, sometimes ever so long after midnight has struck from the two grave old churches whose towers stand dark and square against the sky, like twin warders of the river.

Very merry are these evenings, very full of mirth and wit, nights to be remembered—verily 'society;' curiously different from the stately interchange of civilities among the little-great of suburb or country town, who disseminate dulness at measured intervals, and call it 'visiting.'

The buffet in the little Pompeian dining-room is always liberally furnished. Herman's den serves as a smoking-room, and is sometimes crowded to suffocation with noisy disputants, who can talk louder here than in Mrs. Westray's drawing-room, where the wives are comparing notes about babies with Editha, and repeating the last *mot* from the nursery. Some of the wives and sisters are musical, and there are songs and sonatas and an occasional glee — 'See our oars with feathered spray,' or 'From Oberon in fairyland'—to diversify the evening's entertainment. Curious-looking foreigners, whom Herman picks up at his club, come down occasionally, and draw strange and subtle harmonies from the Broadwood miniature grand. But conversation is the great feature of the assembly. That never flags. Samuel Johnson and his chosen circle never discussed a wider range of topics, never soared to the immensities or descended to the trivialities, with bolder wing than Mr. Westray and his friends. Barkly Tollemy often exhibits his tall figure and wise gray head among the younger guests, and discusses the various problems of a phenomenal universe with Herman, or gives utterance to the most scathing criticisms with an unctuous humour that makes the sharpest words seem sweet as honey. Editha has left off listening to the metaphysical arguments. She is happy in having Herman near her, in seeing him pleased and amused, and in knowing that at least for this one night in the week his own house is as attractive to him as Mrs. Brandreth's. True there are people who go to the popular actress who never come here—distinguished members of the patrician order, who think it a favour to be presented to the popular manageress of the Frivolity; famous doctors, famous lawyers, who like to relax the tension of the bow in Myra's pretty drawing-room, and to have their last pet anecdote laughed at by the favourite actress; while Herman, being only an author, is but little sought by the great. But he has the society he likes best, and is satisfied.

The Bordeaux and light German wines, the chicken and anchovy sandwiches, the effervescing waters and old cognac, the tea and coffee and pound cakes and Presburg biscuits, consumed at these weekly réunions cost something; but Editha is too pleased with Herman's pleasure to count the cost, and so life glides on calmly, almost happily, for the young wife, despite those melancholy Sunday evenings when her husband is planning a new play at Kensington Gore.

Among the most constant guests at Mrs. Westray's Tuesdays is Hamilton Lyndhurst. He is such a near neighbour, as he tells Editha, and it is easy for him to drop in. Indeed, he has not waited for the institution of these weekly receptions to become a frequent dropper-in. He has spent many an evening in the little Dutch drawing-room — with its green-damask walls and old delft jars and quaint tulipwood cabinets—furnished after a Dutch picture.

He has contrived somehow to make himself a friend of the family, to subordinate all those characteristics which Herman observed in him at the beginning of their acquaintance, and to get himself, in a manner, rehabilitated in his friend's esteem. Before his marriage Herman had made up his mind that Lyndhurst was one of those desirable bachelor acquaintances who ought to be buried in the grave of a man's bachelorhood; but since his marriage he has come to think that Lyndhurst is a very good fellow after all, with rather too much audacity in expressing his opinions among men, perhaps, but a man of kindly feeling and genuine good-nature, and with a perfect appreciation of good and pure-minded women.

To Editha Mr. Lyndhurst has succeeded in making himself eminently agreeable. He has dropped-in when husband and wife have been alone together in Herman's study, and has contrived to fall into that small domestic circle without causing a break in its unity. He can talk well when he likes, he sings and plays exquisitely, and seems never so well pleased as when Mrs. Westray asks him to go to the piano. That musical genius gives him an elevated air in Editha's mind; she cannot imagine evil in a man who can interpret the great classic composers with such divine expression, and whose deep pathetic voice rises in power and grandeur with the grandeur of his theme.

CHAPTER XI.

> 'Aus dieser Erde quillen meine Freuden,
> Und diese Sonne scheinet meinen Leiden;
> Kann ich mich erst von ihnen scheiden,
> Dann mag, was will und kann, geschehn.'

THE Tuesdays have been established for nearly two months—the London season is over. It is Sunday, late in July, the July of 1870. The Franco-Prussian war has begun, and neutral England is breathless and excited to fever-point, watching that awful contest, and prophesying darkly as to its upshot. Editha is thinking rather sadly of an approaching visit to Lochwithian with her boy; sadly because Herman pleads his literary work as a reason for staying in London, while she goes alone to exhibit her firstborn to the fond and admiring eyes of his aunt and grandfather.

'But surely, dear Herman, you could write better at Lochwithian,' she pleads, when first this bitter fact of his preferring to remain in town is made known to her; 'the pure air, the quiet—'

'My dearest, pray sink that absurd notion about rustic tranquillity. Dogs barking, cocks crowing, guns firing—your father coming in to propose a ride—Mr. Petherick bursting in upon us with the news of some startling event in the village—Betsy Jones has had a letter from her brother in America—or Polly Evans's little boy has set fire to his pinafore. And then there is the temptation which the smiling green hills, and the busy babbling water-falls, and the glad blue sky, are always offering a man to go out of doors and be idle and happy. I never could stay long within four walls in the country.'

'But think what good rest and mountain-air would do your health, Herman,' replies Editha anxiously.

'My love, it is not a question of health, but of getting my book finished within a given time,' he answers, somewhat impatiently. 'I can work nowhere so well as in this little room. Molding and Korness may have charged rather dear for their notions of comfort, but they have certainly succeeded in making me comfortable. This den is the dearest place in the world, and when you and the little one are here, a domestic Eden.'

The tender speech, coming upon her in the midst of her disappointment, moves Editha almost to tears. She takes up her husband's hand and kisses it.

'Dear hand, which works so hard for baby and me!' she exclaims.

Herman draws her to him with a sigh.

'Dear love, I have worked hard enough, but perhaps I have not been quite so prudent as I ought to have been. I am not saving money, and a man who has given hostages to Fortune should have his modest share of the Three per Cents.'

'But you are not in difficulties, Herman?' Editha inquires anxiously.

'No, dear, not in difficulties,' he answers, with a faint gulp, as if conscience were swallowing a pill. 'I am only a little anxious about your future and the little one's if—if anything were to happen to me; like poor Mandeville for instance.'

Mandeville is a writer of promise who has perished untimely, leaving a wife and children, and not so much as a scuttle of coals or a bundle of firewood in his house.

'Herman, don't talk of such a thing!' cries Editha, pale with agony at the suggestion that her beloved is mortal.

'No, dear, it is not a thing to talk about; but it is a thing that a man can't help thinking about now and then, when he looks in the faces of his children and remembers how brief a journey it must be for them from his deathbed to the workhouse.'

'Then we are living beyond our means, Herman!' exclaims Editha. 'Why did you not tell me this sooner? I will do anything, dear—economise in any way you like—send away one of the servants, or two even—remove to a smaller house.'

'My dearest, I don't want to advertise to the world just yet that I am a failure. This house suits us to a nicety. Your present cook seems a very decent person. All I have to do is to stick close to my work, and to go on being successful. I shall be afraid even to speak seriously to you, darling, if you take fright so quickly.'

'I am only distressed to think that you should have worked so hard, and that we should have squandered all your earnings upon servants and dinner-parties, carriages and horses. We can get rid of that last expense at any rate, Herman. You bought the carriages and horses to please me. I can do without them very well indeed, dear—so you can sell them as soon as you like.'

'You don't know what you are talking about, love. A man may buy horses and carriages—some people even go so far as to consider that an improvident proceeding—but he can't sell them. That means throwing his money into the gutter.'

'But to get rid of the expense of keeping them, Herman; that would be an advantage, even if you lost ever so much by selling them.'

'When ruin is staring us in the face we'll think of it, dear,' answers Herman carelessly, but with a touch of weariness in tone and manner, like a man who feels himself overweighted in the universal handicap.

It is not from lack of love for wife and child that Herman shrinks from accompanying them to Lochwithian. He has a sense of anxiety which makes him recoil from the idea of rural tranquillity and calm autumn days. He is overworked, and knows it; yet is anxious to write faster than ever—to achieve some striking success, dramatic or literary, in order to be once more in advance of Fortune. He is glad to avoid the risk of friendly and confidential converse with the Squire, who might ask him searching questions about his affairs. A certain irritability, which has been growing upon him of late, seems to find its best solace in the intellectual atmosphere of his club, or Myra's drawing-room, which is only an elegant reduction of club society; the same men, the same subjects of conversation, the same tone of being ever so far in advance of the foremost rank of commonplace humanity.

The thing which Herman Westray feels most keenly—perhaps the lurking cause of his fretfulness and discontent—is that invention begins to flag, or even to fail. The crowd of images, the wealth of incident, the variety of subject, which used to throng the chambers of his mind, inhabit there no longer. He is obliged to resort to other men's invention for suggestions that may assist his wearied fancy, and with this view reads innumerable French and German novels, in the majority of which he finds agreeable varieties of stories that have been told a hundred times before, and in the residue no stories at all. Seldom now can he give himself up to the study of those great masters of style, whose imperishable works used to be the delight of his leisure. Actual leisure he has none, and his days of absolute weariness and exhaustion he employs in groping for some available notion in the kennels of continental fiction—a novel which he can condense and crystallise into a drama, or a drama which he can develop and widen into a novel. This sense of the absolute need of incessant work is his excuse to himself for letting Editha pay her home visit alone. That pained and disappointed look of hers haunts him long after his announcement of this intention, but, though it grieves him sorely, it does not induce him to alter his plans.

So Editha leaves the gray old church on this late summer evening more out of spirits than she has felt for a long time. All through the bright busy

London season, when her husband has spent so much of his time away from her, she has looked forward to the autumn visit to Lochwithian, consoling herself with that sweet home picture of the idle days they are to spend together in the fair harvest month. She has spanned the gulf between the dreary present and the happy future with hope's golden bridge, as the sea-king in the old German ballad bridged over the waters that severed him from his earth-born love. Thus the disappointment is more bitter even than disappointment is wont to be, and all through this evening's sermon, in the fading summer light, she has been taking a despondent view of life, and agreeing heartily with the preacher, who quotes the wise saying of Sir Thomas Brown to the effect that this world is not an inn, but a hospital.

Alone in the declining light she leaves the old church, and returns to the home which seems so empty without Herman. He is dining at Mrs. Brandreth's, where he is to meet some new star in the literary heaven—an American poet, whose wild strong verse has caught the English ear with its vigorous melody. She might have gone with him, she knows, had she so chosen, and can therefore hardly consider his absence an unkindness. Yet she feels that the early sweetness of their wedded life is gone, and that she can scarcely be first in her husband's thoughts when he holds it too great a sacrifice to give up a Sunday dinner-party for her sake. She makes her sacrifice uncomplainingly for the sake of principle, for the faith in which she has been brought up, whose simple rules and ordinances seem puritanical to Herman's easy way of thinking.

A gentleman is waiting at the little gate of Bridge-end House as she approaches—a tall and large gentleman, with dark eyes, and a face which, although not so young as it has been, is still eminently handsome.

'How do you do, Mr. Lyndhurst? Have you been ringing?' Editha asks, as she shakes hands with this evening visitor.

'Two or three times,' replies Lyndhurst carelessly; 'but your people seem afflicted with temporary deafness. I daresay they are watching the steamers. There's generally one aground for two or three hours on a Sunday evening hereabouts—amusing, rather, for the spectators. The grounded ones usually sing hymns or dance the varsoviana, I believe, to beguile the time. You never heard of the varsoviana, perhaps, Mrs. Westray. It is a dance known in the dark ages, before the Indian Mutiny, and still affected by the lower classes.' And so talking, Mr. Lyndhurst follows Editha into the house, the parlour-maid having been recalled to a consciousness of her duties by this time.

The house has a deserted look on this summer Sabbath evening. The light is dying in the saffron west, and the corners of the room are shadowy.

'Don't ring for lamps on my account, Mrs. Westray,' says Lyndhurst, as Editha lays her hand on the bell. 'This July twilight is delicious.'

'Yes, there is a lovely calmness in this faint gray light,' she answers, seating herself in a low chair in the balcony, which at this season is like a part of the room. 'But it is rather melancholy, at least when one is—'

'Already disposed to sadness?' hazards Lyndhurst.

'I did not quite mean that. When one is alone.'

'True,' he answers gravely. 'Solitude is only tolerable to the man who has nothing to regret. Nay, for the man who does regret there is no such thing as solitude. His loneliness is peopled with phantoms.'

Editha sighs. Her lonely hours have their ghost. They are haunted by the memory of happier days.

'You are thinking of leaving town soon, I suppose?' asks Mr. Lyndhurst. It is the stereotyped question just now.

'Almost immediately. Baby and I are going to Wales next week, to stay with my father.'

'Baby and you, and baby's papa, of course,' remarks Mr. Lyndhurst, with supreme innocence, having only yesterday at his club distinctly heard Herman say that he was too hard at work to take his wife into the country.

'No, I am sorry to say Herman is not able to go with us. He is so anxious about his literary engagements. He has a commission for a new comedy, to be produced early in the winter.'

'At the Frivolity?'

'No. His last piece is likely to run for a year, I believe.'

'He is lucky in having such an actress as Mrs. Brandreth. Wonderful woman; gifted in every way.'

'Yes, she is very clever, and very fascinating.'

'Charming, isn't she? Artificial, of course. She would never have taken such a brilliant position if she were not artificial. And when art is so delightful, why should one languish for nature?'

'She struck me as spontaneous in her acting.'

'Yes, she has her sudden flashes of passion, like Edmund Kean. But underlying all that seems spontaneous there is a mathematical knowledge of effect. She can calculate the force and pressure of her art to a hair. Curious that a simple girl, brought up, not amongst the lamps and sawdust, but in a quiet Devonshire village, should develop into such an artist.'

'Devonshire!' repeats Editha curiously. 'Does Mrs. Brandreth come from Devonshire?'

'Didn't you know that?'

'No, indeed. I had no idea that she was a countrywoman of Herman's.'

Lyndhurst looks at her for a few moments thoughtfully, as if he were weighing some question in his mind, and then replies in his most careless tone. He might tell her something about her husband's past which would sting her to the quick; but it strikes him that the time is not yet ripe for him to impart that piece of information. He has his fuse ready, whenever he cares to use it, but is in no hurry to spring the mine.

'Well, I am not sure that she is a native, but I know she was brought up in the West of England. Are you fond of the drama, Mrs. Westray? Do you like your husband to write for the stage?'

'I like him to be successful in his art,' she answers, 'and to follow the natural bent of his genius. But I sometimes think that he would be happier if he wrote only books. He is too anxious for the success of his plays, too much elated by triumph, too much depressed by failure. A book can afford to wait for praise and recognition, but a play—'

'Assails Fortune like a highwayman, demanding your money or your life,' says Lyndhurst, laughing. 'I always pity the unhappy author on those brilliant first nights, when all intellectual London is on the alert, quite as ready to hiss a defeat as to applaud a success. One sees the wretched being who has set the puppets in motion writhing in the stalls, or smiling with a dolorous smile at those jokes which he thought would set the house in a roar, and which nobody sees. How flat his impassioned speeches seem to fall—what weaknesses he sees in the fabric of his play to-night, which never struck him at rehearsal! How keenly those agonised eyes of his examine the faces of the critics, inscrutable as the Sphinx! And when a man in the gallery laughs in the right place, he could hug that man in a gush of gratitude. No, Mrs. Westray, I do not envy the dramatist his rare triumphs. Your husband must be working rather too hard, by the way, when he cannot afford himself an autumnal holiday, were it ever so brief.'

'Yes,' answers Editha with a sigh, 'it has been a great disappointment to all of us. I think even baby understands, and is sorry papa is not going into the country with him.'

'Intelligent baby! I suppose the little one is not on view so late in the evening? I should have liked to see what progress he has made since he and I made friends in the early summer.'

Mr. Lyndhurst on one of his friendly visits has been introduced to baby, and has contrived to fascinate that young member of the household. There are men whom children, horses, and dogs are attracted to; not always the best men, perhaps. Is it not rather a question of animal magnetism than superlative virtue, this influence which man exercises over the lesser brutes?

'Baby has been fast asleep for ever so long, I hope. Herman is dining with Mrs. Brandreth, to meet Mr. Molony, the American poet. I wonder you are not there.'

'Mrs. Brandreth was kind enough to ask me, and her Sunday evenings are charming. But there are times when one is not quite in tune with that kind of thing; times when a solitary ramble in the lanes about Wimbledon Common is better than brillant society and a file-firing of epigrams. I enjoy half-an-hour's quiet chat like this more than the loudest roaring of Mrs. Brandreth's literary lions.'

'It is good of you to enliven my solitude for a little while,' replies Editha, who is really cheered by this friendly talk in the twilit balcony, and whose innocence has no knowledge of Mr. Lyndhurst's evil repute. She knows he is her husband's friend, and accepts that fact as a certificate of character. 'I wonder you do not go to Mrs. Brandreth's for the sake of the music,' she adds. 'Herman tells me there is often first-rate music.'

'Some of the best, doubtless; but do not think me egotistical if I confess that I would rather play one of Beethoven's sonatas to myself, in a half-dark room like this, than hear it performed a great deal better amidst the half-whispered chit-chat of a parcel of people of whom about one in ten knows what is being played, while one in twenty cares about it.'

'You play so well that you can afford to say that.'

'I think I should feel it if I could not play at

all. I would hire some half-starved professor—an unappreciated genius—to play Beethoven and Mozart for me between the lights, while I smoked my pipe. Music to the man or woman who cares for it is better than opium-eating. Your true musician sees as many visions as were ever beheld by Coleridge or De Quincey.'

'If he starts with as rich an imagination as Coleridge or De Quincey. A man's own mind must create his dream pictures. Opium or music can only set the machinery in motion.'

'True, Mrs. Westray. In that case I am not without imagination. I know there are times when my fancy is a daring one.'

Something in his tone, which sinks to deeper earnestness with this last sentence, might give the alarm to a woman of the world; but to Editha it conveys nothing beyond the idea that Mr. Lyndhurst has more sentiment, or even romance, in his composition than she has given him credit for.

'It is curious that you should be going to Wales,' he says presently, after a pause, in which they have both looked dreamily at the river.

'Curious that I am going to my father's house!' she exclaims wonderingly.

'Ah, to be sure; I forgot that. I meant that it was curious you should be going to Wales just now. My doctor has ordered me to drink the sulphur water at a place with an odd name—let me see—Llandrysak, I think it is called.'

'That is within ten miles of Lochwithian, my father's place. How curious!'

'Odd, isn't it?'

'Very; but I believe the doctors are beginning to think a good deal of the Llandrysak springs. Herman was sent there for his health three years ago.'

'And it was by that hazard he met you? Happy man to find a treasure even greater than health! If every sick Numa could discover such an Egeria at the spring he is sent to, water cure would be your only remedy.'

'I am sorry to hear you are ill enough to be sent to Llandrysak,' says Editha.

'Ill!' he repeats rather vacantly. 'O, it is not absolute illness! Want of tone, the doctors call it;

or in other words, a fatal tendency towards old age. However, I expect the Welsh waters to make me young again. May I do myself the pleasure of calling on Mr. Morcombe, since I am to be so near? I have already made his acquaintance, you know, here at a very agreeable dinner-party.'

'Ah, I remember you met papa here. I have no doubt he'll be pleased to see you again,' says Editha, with galling indifference; and then remembering Mr. Lyndhurst's one sublime power, she adds, with more interest, 'I should like to introduce you to my sister, and for her to hear you play, if possible. She is an invalid, and rarely has the pleasure of hearing good music.'

'Except when you play to her.'

'I! O, my powers are very small in that way. I can play just well enough to please and soothe poor Ruth, when there is no better music to be had.'

Evening has deepened into night by this time —summer stars peeping out of the shadowy summer sky; the lights of Putney shining through the river mists; one lazy boat moving gently with the stream, the oars resting in the rullocks, the oarsmen singing softly as they drift. Mr. Lyndhurst feels that to prolong his visit would be an impertinence.

'Good-bye, Mrs. Westray; I'll go and smoke my cigar in the Wimbledon lanes. At least I won't say good-bye, but *au revoir*, in the hope of seeing you at Lochwithian.' And thus they shake hands and part, and it seems to Hamilton Lyndhurst that he is voluntarily departing out of paradise. Perhaps in the worst men's minds there is some latent capacity for pure feeling, and in the worst men's lives one love which is not all unholy. Or say rather that through the dark veil that shuts these evil natures from the good man's heaven there flashes an occasional ray of light. They are capable of feeling as tender a reverence for virtue as Faust felt beside Gretchen's pillow, and they are capable of sinning as Faust sinned against the woman whose purity can move them to tears.

Hamilton Lyndhurst reviews his career that night as he smokes the pipe of contemplation in the Wimbledon lanes, and he tells himself that his life and his character might have been different had he met such a woman as Editha ten years earlier.

'I am the kind of man who must be happy at any price,' he says to himself; 'but happiness would have been none the less sweet to me if I had found it in the paths of virtue. Vice in the abstract has no attraction for me. I have admired and pursued worthless women, knowing them worthless; but I never loved such an one. With me vice has been another name for convenience. Till I saw Westray's wife I never met with a woman worth the sacrifice of matrimony.'

Despite his sentimental talk with Editha of quiet evenings and the pleasures of solitude, there is nothing rarer in Mr. Lyndhurst's life than loneliness and self-inspection. He lives like a wealthy profligate in imperial Rome, surrounded with his little circle of parasites, flatterers, and flute-players. If he is weary or out of spirits, his mountebanks and jesters bring forth their treasures of wit and buffoonery for his diversion, his flute-players pipe their sweetest and smile their brightest to beguile him from thought or sadness. Thus he has hardly time to discover that his life is as foolish as it is worthless; that his evil influence upon others whom his wealth corrupts or his selfishness destroys is even less than his evil influence upon himself.

Of late the flute-players, parasites, and flatterers have found their lord and patron less amusable than of old. He has changed his bosom friend once in six months, instead of once in two years. He has given fewer dinners, has not driven his chosen set to Virginia Water once in the season that is just over, and has displayed unmitigated weariness at those banquets at Greenwich and Richmond which have been eaten at his cost. His team of bays and their attendant gooms have had an easy time of it this year; for, except to put in an appearance at Hyde-Park Corner on field-days, Mr. Lyndhurst has made little use of his drag. The mail phaeton, with the tall chestnuts, has been altogether idle, Mr. Lyndhurst spending his leisure for the most part in lounging about his Walham-Green garden, where there is a spacious shrubbery-surrounded lawn, enriched with three of those fine old cedars which are still to be found in this south-western suburb. It is a garden as completely hidden from the outer world as if it were a clearing in the Australian Bush; and here Hamilton Lyndhurst, stretched at ease upon the velvet sward, in smoking-jacket and slippers, reads the newspapers, or dozes over a French novel on sultry summer mornings, till it is time to dress and repair to the clubs or the City, where he disposes of his afternoon either in gossip or business, winding up with a little dinner at club or restaurant, and finishing his evening in haunts known to his species, and to no other section of humanity.

The flute-players and parasites, perceiving this change in their city Sardanapalus, lay their heads together and hold counsel as to the cause. The parasites opine that their patron has been losing money; has been hard hit, has come to grief in one of those commercial steeplechases in which the riders make a short cut to wealth through other people's fortunes. The flute-players sigh, and suggest that Mr. Lyndhurst may have fallen in love. The chief parasite laughs, or in his own vernacular 'screams,' at the notion.

'He has been falling in love once in six months or so for the last fifteen years,' says this gentleman; 'and did you ever know his last infatuation put him out of sorts? He is like Bussy Rabutin, he takes the fever lightly. Depend upon it, the source of his gloom is in the House, and not in the heart.'

'Perhaps he is tired of us,' speculates one of the flute-players. 'He is sometimes barely civil, and he forgot to send me the gloves I won at Goodwood. At least, I'm not quite clear that I won them, but I know I asked him to send them to me—lavender and apricot, four buttons. I wanted them quite awfully.'

'A bad sign, that sort of thing, no doubt; but if we bored him he would give us the sack. No man has a more placid way of letting his dear friends know they're out of fashion.'

'True,' sighs the damsel; 'poor Florence Montmorency almost broke her heart at his treatment.'

'She did more,' replies the parasite; 'she put down her brougham.'

Thus argue Mr. Lyndhurst's friends, while the subject of their discourse goes his way, unhappy, yet not altogether hopeless. A man who for fifteen years has commanded all prizes that Fortune can give is hardly to be persuaded, save by the experience of absolute failure, that life holds anything quite out of his reach. Hamilton Lyndhurst is the spoiled child of a money-making age; an age in which the power of wealth overrides every other potentiality; an age of gold, in which rank and ancient race have dwindled from their place, or have voluntarily cast themselves down before the chariot of a gilded Juggernaut.

Hamilton Lyndhurst is one of those men for whom good luck seems to be an inheritance. Manhood brought him no estate save his brains, but he has been what his intimates call 'in the swim' from the very beginning of his career. He is a man who turns all he touches to gold; or who, touching anything not so convertible, lets it go again so quickly as to escape impoverishment from the contact. He is in and out of a hazardous speculation before the general public have quite made up their minds about it; but to whatever dismal depth of discount the shares in that speculation eventually descend, they are sure to be above par just in that halcyon week when Mr. Lyndhurst sells out. Clergymen's widows and speculative spinsters may bemoan the collapse of that bubble into which their little capitals have melted, but however brief the delusion Mr. Lyndhurst has awakened in time to retire advantageously. Touch and go has been the ruling principle of all his operations. He is the Proteus of the Stock Exchange, and those who know him best, and regulate their own ventures by his genius, may have some idea of his operations to-day, but cannot venture a guess as to his transactions to-morrow. And thus, having ridden on the shoulders of Fortune as on a horse; having been lucky himself, and the source of luck in others; having been flattered, followed, and caressed from youth to middle age, never having encountered the mind which his wealth could not influence, or the rectitude which it could not corrupt, the idea of failure in any enterprise he may undertake, however wicked or however perilous, finds no place in Hamilton Lyndhurst's thoughts. He sees Editha Westray the devoted wife of another man, and, undaunted, unabashed by her purity, tells himself that she is just the one woman who could redeem his existence from vapid profligacy and stale pleasures, and open for him the gates of that unknown world of placid domesticity which, seen from afar, seems to him the wearied profligate's natural haven of rest. He tells himself furthermore that there is no legal process in the land more common than the loosening of marriage bonds, and sets himself to consider by what concatenation of circumstances Editha might be divorced from the husband who so poorly appreciates her peerless worth, and be rendered free to bless the man who knows her value.

Mr. Lyndhurst has seen Herman at Mrs. Brandreth's very often of late, has observed their confidential converse, which may or may not be flirtation, but which assuredly has a sentimental air. Those evenings spent in Myra's drawing-room appear to Mr. Lyndhurst an evidence of Herman's weariness at home. The golden days are over; the husband finds another woman more amusing than his wife, and that other the woman he once loved. Lyndhurst has had the secret of that early attachment from Myra's own lips, in one of those fits of despair in which a woman must have a confidant, however dangerous.

Unhappily, no sin of Herman's—were he to exuberate from foolishness into sin—would loosen the legal tie. He is not likely to assail his wife to the endangerment of life or limb in the presence of witnesses, and only by absolute cruelty can he forfeit the right to be, by law, her husband. On this side Mr. Lyndhurst sees no hope. But the wife, by one rash act, by one fatal unpremeditated step, by folly that should look like sin—nay, with perfect innocence of act and intention, betrayed into some false position by the treachery of others, netted and trapped like a snared bird—might snap the chain which a masculine legislature has contrived to make so brittle for woman, so strong for man.

Dark and cloudy are Hamilton Lyndhurst's ideas at present; vague and shadowy the visions of his head upon his bed. But Editha's is the one image that occupies his reveries and haunts his dreams, and all his thoughts tend one way.

It is just possible that he might have ceased to think of one whose purity and fidelity would seem to place her in a region beyond the hopes of the most audacious dreamer if his thoughts had been allowed to follow their own bent, uninfluenced by subtle suggestions from another. True that he is a bold bad man; a man who has said to himself with Satan, 'Evil, be thou my good;' a man who believes in nothing, hopes for nothing, fears nothing, beyond this imperceptible spot upon the face of nature which we call the world. Yet even the most unscrupulous sinner recoils before the beauty of absolute purity, and Hamilton Lyndhurst might have reconciled himself to the fact that here was one woman utterly beyond reach of temptation, had he not been stimulated to hopefulness by the voice of the tempter.

The tempter speaks in the accents of Myra Brandreth, who takes care to inform Mr. Lyndhurst from time to time of Herman's moral deterioration; how he has grown weary of domesticity already, and is never so happy as when away from home; how Mrs. Westray is evidently—a useful word, and of widest significance, that evidently—unappreciated and neglected. A pity; so young and lovely a creature; but rather dull, Mrs. Brandreth opines, and hardly a fitting companion for Herman.

'You ought to have married him,' says Mr. Lyndhurst.

Myra sighs.

'I think we should have suited each other,' she answers, with placid melancholy.

As one confidence deserves another, Mr. Lyndhurst lets her into the secret of his intense admiration for Mrs. Westray. He describes that feeling as a sentiment of exquisite purity, the worship of some bright particular star, rather than admiration of another man's wife. Myra sympathises abundantly, and is all the more sorry for Mr. Lyndhurst's hopeless passion because the lady who inspires it is so unhappy in her union with Herman Westray.

'A literary man should never marry at all,' says Mrs. Brandreth conclusively. 'He is too self-absorbed, too dependent on the sunshine of the hour, to make a good husband. Or if he must marry, he should at least choose a wife who can help him in his art.'

'As you help Westray,' suggests Lyndhurst, with his subtle smile. 'However dear his wife may be to him as the sharer of his home, you are the partner of his dramatic successes, and have exercised the greater influence on his career.'

Myra sighs again, a deprecating sigh this time,

as if she would fain dispute the statement were it not so obviously true. And thus, the subject of conversation between two utterly unscrupulous people, who have never acknowledged any higher law than their own inclinations, Editha may be said to walk blindfold in paths of danger.

CHAPTER XII.

'But Faustus' offence can ne'er be pardoned; the serpent that tempted Eve may be saved, but not Faustus.'

HOME, a peaceful land smiling in the ripening harvest sunshine. How sweet it is to Editha, returning to her old life, surrounded by the old faces, as in the days that are gone—so utterly gone, so far away even in her memory, that she almost wonders at finding little change in the familiar scenes and faces of her youth! Not a flower in the garden but blooms as when the garden was her peculiar care; but in herself there is a change as of half a century's experience of life and its bitterness. Not for worlds would she confess, even to herself, that she has been mistaken in her choice or unhappy in her wedded life; but looking back at the last year, from the stand-point of peace and home, she knows that it has been full of care.

She feels that her arrival without Herman is a

disappointment and a cause of wonder for everybody at Lochwithian. Ruth says little, careful not to wound, and seems quite satisfied with Editha's excuses for her husband; but the Squire, outspoken and not richly endowed with tact, talks a good deal about his son-in-law's absence, and in a manner that wounds Editha to the quick.

'I never supposed that a daughter of mine would have had to travel two hundred miles with only a chit of a nursemaid to take care of her. If you had told me that your husband couldn't bring you, I'd have come up to London to fetch you.'

'Indeed, dear papa, there was not the least occasion for your doing so. I could travel much farther with nurse and baby without inconvenience.'

'It's lucky for you that you're so strong-minded,' replies the father grumpily; 'for you've married a man who doesn't seem inclined to give himself much trouble in taking care of you. Things would have been vastly different if you had married Vivian Hetheridge—poor young fellow, not married yet, and broken-hearted about you, every one says.'

'O papa, I saw him last Christmas, and he

has grown ever so stout, and looked wonderfully well.'

'A man may gain weight in spite of his broken heart. A fellow who gets a disappointment of that kind often drops his hunting, and eats and drinks more than is good for him—grows careless about gaining flesh, and goes to the bad altogether. If Hetheridge had got over your treatment of him he'd have married before now. A man with such an estate as his is bound to marry. Ah, how nice it would have been to have you within a ten-mile ride of us!'

'Come, papa, I think you have quite enough of me, taking my half-yearly visits into consideration. See how serious you've made baby look. He is wondering what you are talking about.'

The Squire, who has had too many grandchildren to consider the relationship a privilege, pokes his finger into the infant's chubby neck, and chirrups inanely.

Wherever Editha goes, whomsoever she sees, she has to answer the same inquiries about her absent husband. Her marriage with the popular young writer has been regarded as a small romance in its way, a love-match pure and simple, and people expect to see husband and wife inseparable, an idyllic pair of lovers unspoiled by matrimony. Thus every one is disappointed, and regards Herman's non-appearance as a kind of defection. Mr. Petherick shakes his head and frowns gravely.

'Hard at work at a new play, is he? You shouldn't let him work so hard—wear out his brain, exhaust his constitution; make him old before his time,' he says seriously.

'Indeed, dear Mr. Petherick, I have been most anxious that he should take more rest; but he is in such a hurry to make a fortune for baby.'

'Fortunes are never made in a hurry, my dear. It is the tortoise who gets rich, not the hare.'

'Then I fear Herman will never be rich. There is nothing of the plodder in his nature.'

'So much the worse for both of you,' retorts Mr. Petherick. 'Show me the man who can plod, and I'll show you the man who will succeed. Your lively geniuses, who make a premature success and end in failure, pretend to associate patient industry with dulness; but that idea is only one of those self-sustaining delusions with which idlers console themselves.'

'His worst enemy could not accuse Herman of idleness,' replies Editha. 'I doubt if Mr. Shinebarr, the Queen's Counsel, works harder.'

'Does he work with method?' interrogates the Incumbent significantly; and to this question Mrs. Westray is slow to reply, for her husband's literary labour has of late grown more and more fitful and disorderly. He has written for ten hours at a stretch one day, and abandoned his desk altogether on the next, at the call of some one of those various excuses for waste of time which the world misnames pleasure. He has worked from midnight till morning on a Monday, and has spent Tuesday stretched on a sofa reading a French novel, in the last stage of lassitude. He has deserted his study for a week, and then shut himself up there for days and nights in succession, like Balzac, writing as if driven by Furies; the ultimate result of these spasmodic labours being a less amount of work done than in the calm first year of his married life, when he spent his mornings from eleven till two, and his evenings from nine till eleven, in the domestic retirement of his den, Editha working or reading by fireside or window. Latterly he has been only able to write when alone. The watchful eyes of love have disconcerted him.

Even Mrs. Gredby has something to say about the absent husband when Editha goes to see her. Mrs. Westray drives to the New Inn in a basket pony-carriage with nurse and baby, which latter small individual has to be introduced to every hill and valley, copse and rivulet, wood and meadow, familiar to his mother's girlhood.

'And where's the young gentleman from London?' asks Mrs. Gredby when she has done admiring the baby, whom she regards as an infant prodigy, and who curiously enough shows himself most graciously disposed both to Mrs. Gredby and Mrs. Gredby's old gentleman in the chimney-corner—an infant who has met the advances of the county families with contumely. 'And why didn't he drive over from the Priory with you this fine morning?'

Editha explains.

'I should have thought that people could write

books anywheres,' remarks Mrs. Gredby, 'purvided they'd a bottle of ink, a penn'orth of steel nibs, and a quire of letter-paper. It do seem hard for you to be down here without your husband. Such a loving couple as you looked, too, that day you brought him to see me. But, to be sure, that was before you was married. I haven't worn my Paisley shawl but once since your wedding-day, Miss Editha, and that was at Llanryddyth Eisteddfod last July. And there sits my old gentleman; no change in him, is there? He's looked ready for his coffin for the last ten years; but except rheumatics in every joint, there's not much the matter with him.'

This cheering statement being repeated in a louder key, the old gentleman nods assent thereto blithely.

'No, there ain't much amiss with me except rheumatics,' he says. 'Lord forbid I should repine against Providence; but if we must be made with so many jints, it seems a little hard upon us that we ain't purvided with a larger supply of ile to keep 'em going. But we've all got our burdens. My father had a hassmer, and that were a deal worse; his pore old lungs were that weak as he couldn't reach up to the shelf for his pipe without panting as if he were a-goin' to choke; and I'm sure the noises he made of a hevening was ekal in variety to a band o' wind hinstruments. I haven't had much use in my limbs the last two winters, but my lungs is sound, and I can enjoy my bit o' baccy. The missus is hearty enough; though she's a-growing the box for her grave in our back garding.'

'How do I know that anybody else would take the trouble to grow it for me?' remarks Mrs. Gredby briskly; 'there's nothing like looking arter your own affairs if you want 'em attended to. I shall be under no compliment to neighbours for the box coffin a-top o' my grave; and the thought of that will be a comfort to me as I lie in it,' adds the independent-minded mistress of the New Inn.

There is one change which Editha perceives at Lochwithian, and it is one that pierces her heart, for it is a change for the worse in Ruth. The beautiful face is more delicate, more ethereal than when Editha saw it six months ago. The white hand is more transparent in its ivory pallor. The dark eyes are larger and more lustrous. This chrysalis of mortality perishes and shrinks as that butterfly, the immortal spirit, expands its heavenward-soaring wings. To those who read aright, Ruth wears the stamp of a creature in process of translation from the earthly to the spiritual.

Yet never has the invalid been more cheerful, more hopeful about herself. She suffers less than of old, reads much, talks much at times, and with delightful animation. Her joy in Editha's presence is unbounded; her only subject of regret is the weakness which renders her long-promised journey to London impossible just now.

'I should so love to see your house, darling,' she says, when the sisters are alone together in the summer dusk, hand clasped in hand, Editha on a low chair by Ruth's pillow. 'I begin to wonder if I shall ever see it. Last year Dr. Davies said next year, and now this summer it is next year still. Well, even next year will come at last, I suppose, and I shall see my pet in her own home, the cleverest of housekeepers.'

'I don't know about clever housekeeping,' Editha

answers ruefully. 'We spend a great deal of money, and I can't quite make out how it goes. Of course everything is very dear, as cook says, and Herman is particular about his dinners, and likes game and fish directly it comes in season. We gave three-and-sixpence a pound for salmon ever so many times in the spring; and as cook fries whitebait very nicely, I ordered a pint for Herman two or three times a week in the season. But even allowing for small extravagances of that kind, I think our housekeeping costs more than it ought.'

Hereupon follows a lengthy and confidential conversation, in which Editha gives Ruth various details of domestic economy, or domestic extravagance. Ruth is shocked at hearing the cost of that small ménage at Fulham, and suggests dishonesty on the part of Mrs. Files. Beer, grocery, butcher's meat, everything costs about double what it ought, as Ruth demonstrates to her sister by a rough-and-ready comparison between the Fulham and Lochwithian bills —therefore Mr. and Mrs. Westray are being cheated.

'It is very dreadful to suspect any one,' says Editha, discomposed by this suggestion.

'It is still worse to encourage dishonesty by wilfully shutting one's eyes to it. Let me find you a young woman who can cook—one of your old pupils, perhaps—and take her back with you.'

'Do you think we could find one who would cook well enough for Herman?' inquires Editha doubtfully.

'Why not? I should not engage an inexperienced person; but I would make it my business to find a woman of unimpeachable character.'

'I had an excellent character with Ann Files,' remarks Editha.

'Had you any character of the person who gave the character?'

'Of course not. The lady was quite a stranger to me.'

'And she wanted to get rid of a bad servant without what people call "unpleasantness." I daresay that's how it was. Let me get you a cook, darling, and if she does not fry whitebait as well as this Ann Files, depend upon it she will reduce your housekeeping expenses by nearly half.'

'That would be indeed a comfort. It sometimes

makes me quite unhappy to think how hard Herman has to work to pay for things that are thrown on the dust-heap—broken china, half-burned coals, and so on. And yet I am always begging Files to be economical, and she assures me that it goes to her heart to waste anything; but the things do get wasted somehow.'

'The cook I get you will not be wasteful, dear. I am so glad we have had this little talk, and that I can be useful to you in some small way.'

Editha is grateful, but is sorely exercised by the thought that Mrs. Files is possibly not so honest as she might be. The idea of having been plundered largely for the last two years; of retrospective wastefulness which might have been avoided had she, Editha, been more careful; the idea of Herman's genius having been compelled to do task-work in order that Ann Files might squander the fruits thereof,—notions such as these present themselves to the young wife's mind in a very painful manner, and she is thoughtful and unhappy for the rest of the evening.

Ruth and Mrs. Jones, the good old Lochwithian

housekeeper, hold a consultation next morning, at which Editha is present. Mrs. Jones knows the history of all the young women within ten miles of the Priory, and can lay her hands on a culinary treasure forthwith. Betsy Evans—not the daughter of Evans the grocer, nor Evans the butcher, nor Evans at the Hill Farm, nor Evans who keeps the Prince Albert Inn—but of another Evans who cobbles. Betsy has been a pupil of Editha's at Lochwithian school, and has since graduated as kitchen-maid under Mrs. Davis at Llanmoel Manor-house.

'Are not kitchen-maids in large houses apt to learn wasteful ways?' inquires Editha, with a vivid recollection of Jane Tubbs, who had budded as a kitchen-maid in Belgrave-square to blossom as a cook at Fulham, and who was in the habit of bringing forward 'the square' as a precedent for every extravagance, such as the expenditure of a pound of lard for the frying of a single sole, or the investment of two pounds of gravy-beef in a small boat of gravy, which would have been flavourless if it had not been one-third Worcester sauce.

'Wasteful!' exclaims Mrs. Jones, horrified.

'Wastefulness was never learned at Llanmoel Manor. Mrs. Davis is a woman who couldn't rest quiet in her bed at night if she thought she had wasted so much as the bread-crumbs off the table-cloth. Her poultry is the finest in Radnorshire, and her hens lay all the winter through.'

It is agreed that Betsy Evans shall be engaged to accompany Mrs. Westray to London, upon whose return to Fulham Mrs. Files is to be dismissed with a month's wages. Mrs. Files will of course be angry and remonstrant at this uncourteous treatment; but if she has been as dishonest as Ruth believes, she is not entitled to much courtesy. Editha is delighted at the idea of keeping house with less money, and sparing her dear Herman in some manner.

'It has gone to my heart to ask him for money so often, knowing how hard he has to work for it,' she says sadly; for she feels that the last year of her wedded life might have been happier but for that strain upon her husband's invention, which has made him at once absent-minded, irritable, and moody by the domestic hearth, and eager for the relief of lively society abroad.

Baby, otherwise George Edward, by which names he has been christened, after his two grandfathers, flourishes marvellously in the clear Welsh air, fresh, life-giving, as it blows over the hill-side sheep-walks, the ferny dells and pine-groves. To see the chubby yearling grow rosy and strong, or to hear his happy voice—shrill and loud—as he crawls or rolls upon the short sweet turf, is a joy for Editha, and to be with Ruth a still deeper delight. Yet this first separation from Herman is a sharper trial than the young wife could have foreseen. Her life is snapped asunder, and the larger half of heart and mind are with her husband. Her health improves in her native air, in the divine repose of a country life; but, even seated by Ruth's couch, her thoughts are with Herman in his study. She sees him careworn and anxious, fretful and excited, writing for bread.

'How I wish he loved the country as I do, Ruth!' she exclaims one day, breaking off from the previous subject of conversation to talk of her husband. 'He' always means Herman in Editha's discourse. 'We should be rich then, with my poor little income and the earnings of one novel a year. No need for him to write plays, or worry himself about dramatic critics. I was thinking to-day, as I looked at that pretty house just under the brow of the hill on the Llandrysak road, what a happy home it might be for Herman and me—such a dear old house and garden, all going to rack and ruin for want of a tenant. How cheaply we might live there—no carriages, no dinner-parties, no expensive amusements, but just the simplest easiest life, such as one can fancy Wordsworth and Southey leading in the Lake country!'

'It would be very nice, darling, if it were possible,' replies Ruth; 'it would make my life more happy than words can tell to have you always near me. And surely Herman would write better face to face with nature.'

Editha shakes her head despondently.

'I have told him so sometimes,' she says; 'but he asks me if Samuel Johnson wrote face to face with nature, or Charles Lamb, or Thackeray, or Dickens. I reminded him once that all our greatest poets have lived remote from cities, at which he laughed and said, "There's a trifling exception to your rule in the person of one William Shakespeare, whose works were for the most part produced in the neighbourhood of Blackfriars, as the dramatic exigences of the Globe Theatre demanded. Ben Jonson, Marlow, Dryden, and a few others were also denizens of the streets." And then he tells me that he is not a poet, but a painter of manners and a recorder of events, and that he must live where men abound and events follow one another quickly.'

'I should have thought that for a man who had seen the world and mingled largely with his fellow-men the repose of a country life would be most of all conducive to thought and invention,' replies Ruth. 'Memory, undisturbed by the distractions of to-day, would reproduce the images and impressions of the past; all that a man had seen, suffered, and felt would appear before him distinctly, as in a picture which he need only copy. I can hardly imagine any man writing a great book amidst the distractions of London society.'

Herman's letters are frequent, but brief and hurried. He writes in a cheerful spirit, however, and begs his wife to be happy, and to obtain all the good she can for herself and baby from the healthful repose of home. 'You were looking worn and harassed when you left me, dearest,' he writes, with all his old tenderness. 'I shall expect to see you return with the roses I admired so much in the young lady who gave the chief prize at the Eisteddfod.'

Editha has been at home nearly a fortnight, and has quite forgotten Mr. Lyndhurst's intention of trying the healing waters of Llandrysak, nothing having yet occurred to remind her of that gentleman's existence. It is a sultry August afternoon— a day on which the world seems to have fallen asleep in the sunshine, and even that sleepy hollow, Lochwithian, is a shade more slumberous than usual. The waters of the Pennant have dwindled to a thread of silver, and trickle gently over those crags adown which they are wont to tumble furiously with the brawl of a small cataract. It is Saturday afternoon, too, and everybody's work seems to be done except Editha's. She and an under-gardener go down to the church together, laden with stephanotis and ferns for the decoration of altar and chancel, reading-desk and font; not that to-morrow is any especial Sunday in the ecclesiastical calendar, but rather because the flowers are in their August prime, and Editha deems their fittest use is in the adornment of her beloved church.

She takes the basket of flowers from the gardener in the porch, dismisses him, and goes in alone. The door of this house of prayer is left open for the most part, Mr. Petherick having a notion that a tired labourer returning from his daily toil may like now and then to enter that shadowy temple and kneel for a little while before the sculptured altar, whose Christian emblems no bishop has yet condemned.

Editha pauses on the threshold, surprised, delighted by the sound of the organ, touched as she has never heard it touched before. Some one, a stranger, is playing Mendelssohn's 'I waited for the Lord,' and the instrument she knows so well is breathing forth tones of sweetness and power that move her almost to tears.

Who can the player be beneath whose skilful hands the organ speaks a new language? Some tourist, no doubt. An occasional tourist, archæologically-minded, finds his way to Lochwithian in the course of a summer, to grope and pry among the foundations of the Priory, and come to arbitrary conclusions about the history thereof.

Mrs. Westray moves softly about her work, listening to the player. He glides from Mendelssohn into the 'Agnus Dei' in Mozart's First Mass in C. The organ, a small one, is on one side of the chancel, screened by purple-silk curtains. Editha is very near the player as she builds a bank of flowers upon the reading-desk, pleased to think of Mr. Petherick's delight to-morrow when he sees her work.

The last notes of the 'Agnus Dei' fade into silence, the invisible stranger strikes a chord, and a deep full voice begins to sing a Latin version of Editha's favourite hymn, 'Rock of Ages.' The voice is Hamilton Lyndhurst's, and she wonders at herself for not having recognised the touch of the musician. No doubt it is because she has never heard him play the organ before.

She goes on with her work noiselessly while he sings. She is wreathing one of the candelabra with stephanotis and long sprays of maiden-hair as Mr. Lyndhurst appears from behind the curtains, and his coming discomposes her no more than if he were the purblind little organist she has known from her childhood. He has quite enough penetration to see this, and is not flattered by the fact. It is new to him to meet a woman to whom his presence is a matter of indifference, and this woman is one upon whom he has bestowed more earnest thought than he has given to the rest of her sex in the aggregate.

He has heard her enter the church, watched her through a chink in the curtains, and has played and sung for her edification.

'How do you like our organ, Mr. Lyndhurst?' she asks as they shake hands.

'Not at all bad for such a small one. I came to Lochwithian with the idea of calling at the Priory, but seeing the church door open strayed in to look at it, and could not resist trying the organ. Fortunate for me, as I can now enter the Priory under your wing.'

'Papa will be very pleased to see you. Have you been long in Wales?'

'I came only yesterday.'

'Indeed! Then you have seen Herman, perhaps, this week?' she says eagerly, delightedly, as if to have seen Herman was to belong to a privileged order of beings.

'How the simpleton loves him!' thinks Lyndhurst, upon whom this single-hearted, all-absorbing affection has no more influence than the plaintive bleating of the foredoomed calf upon its executioner the butcher. He has made up his mind that this one woman can make him happy—can bend the straggling line of his life into a perfect circle, can harmonise an existence which is now chaotic; and with what dishonour he may stain his manhood, what anguish he may inflict upon others ere he reach his aim, is a calculation that has no place in his thoughts.

'Did you see him?' She repeats her question eagerly, wondering at that troubled look which clouds Mr. Lyndhurst's face for a moment.

'Yes; he dined at Mrs. Brandreth's last Sunday. A delightful little dinner. Just seven people, and, with the exception of your humble servant, all distinguished; the kind of society Westray enjoys so thoroughly.'

'Yes,' sighs Editha, 'he is very fond of clever people. Did you think him looking ill—overworked?'

'On the contrary, he was in high spirits, and looked, as I thought, better than usual—younger, brighter, more like the young fellow I remember seven years ago, fresh from Balliol, and full of enthusiasm and belief in the perfectability of human nature. I daresay if I had seen him next morning in his study I should have found a difference. It is the reaction that tells. We did not leave Mrs. Brandreth till the small hours. Rather too bad for a quiet little dinner, wasn't it? So many people dropped in during the evening, and every one had so much to say.'

'I wonder Mrs. Brandreth can support the fatigue of those Sunday evenings, after acting six nights a week.'

'Do you? That shows how little you know her. She is a creature who lives upon excitement, as a Malay upon opium. Give her leisure for thought, and she would die in a year.'

'Are her thoughts so bitter that she could not bear them?'

They have come out into the little garden-like churchyard, and linger, Mr. Lyndhurst looking rather absently at the tombstones as he talks.

'I think she has had her disappointments—perhaps I ought rather to say disappointment; for you know in my creed intense feeling comes but once in a life.'

'She was left a widow so early,' says Editha compassionately.

'Ye-es,' drawls Lyndhurst; 'but I doubt if the loss of Captain Brandreth sits very heavily on her spirit.'

'Was he not a good man?'

'Good? Not in the church-going sense, I fear; but he was thoroughly harmless. A well-meaning young man, who carried a bull-terrier in his coat-pocket and gave his mind to billiards. Nobody's enemy but his own, and very much his own. He was of a good family, and had expectations. Myra Clitheroe married the expectations, which were nipped untimely by his death. I daresay that notion worries her a little.'

Editha looks grave. She and Myra have never

fraternised, and she likes her less after this hasty sketch of Mr. Lyndhurst's.

'I am glad you thought him looking well,' she remarks, recurring to Herman.

'Poets always look well by lamplight. Have you seen his verses in the new weekly journal, the *Connoisseur?*'

'Verses? No, indeed. He so seldom writes poetry, though he is by nature a poet. Is there a poem of his in the *Connoisseur?* And he has not sent it to me! How cruel!'

'Perhaps he thinks it a little out of your line. The *Connoisseur* people wanted him to do something for their first number, so he dashed off half-a-dozen verses; and the little *tour de force* has made quite a hit. Every one was talking of it at Brandreth's the other night.'

'And I have not seen it!' says Editha, chagrined.

'Old story of the shoemaker's wife, you know. I can bring you the paper to-morrow, or send my groom over with it to-night, if you'd really like to see it.'

'I shall be so much obliged. What is the name of the poem?'

'"Ananke." The word Claude Frollo cut upon the wall of his cell, you know, which in plain English means Fate. The title in Greek characters looks rather *chic*, I assure you. De Musset never did anything better than the poem. The *Connoisseur* is going in for that kind of thing—abuses everybody, hits out from the shoulder right and left, and promises to be a success. I hear there are two injunctions and three actions for libel against the proprietors already; but as the shareholders include two of our wealthiest noblemen and a great City swell, that kind of thing won't balk them. I have pledged myself to support the paper to the extent of a few thousands.'

Editha's interest in the *Connoisseur* is bounded by that one column which contains her husband's verses. Mr. Lyndhurst perceives this, and does not pursue the subject. They pass from the churchyard to the shrubbery, and take the winding path to the house. It is nearly time for afternoon tea in Ruth's room, and Editha means to offer Mr. Lyndhurst that innocent refection. They ascend the shrubberied slope side by side in friendly converse.

It is like Red Ridinghood showing the wolf the way to her grandam's cottage.

'What do you think of Westray's continental expedition?' Lyndhurst inquires presently.

'Continental expedition! I don't know what you mean,' falters Editha, with an alarmed look.

'Perhaps I oughtn't to have mentioned it. After all, it may be only an idea. But I thought he would have told you all about it.'

'About what?'

'The proprietors of his old paper, the *Day Star*, want him to go as special war-correspondent for this Franco-Prussian scrimmage. The man who has been doing the work has knocked under, and come home invalided. They offer Westray splendid terms, and he seems to think the thing would suit him—the variety and excitement freshen his brains, and so on. I daresay he feels himself a little used up after the pace he has been going—in literature, I mean—for the last two years.'

This remark comes like a stab. The last two years are his married life. It is for her sake, for the maintenance of that expensive ill-managed home, he has squandered the wealth of his brain, wasted his genius on recklessly rapid composition. The delicate flowers of his fancy have been forced to premature growth, and their price has gone to fill Ann Files's grease-pot.

This bitter thought gives way before the appalling ideas conjured up by that word 'war-correspondent.' A man who writes history at the cannon's mouth, amidst a hailstorm of shrapnell and grape, with murderous shells tearing up the earth round about him, with new-made chasms yawning before his feet, and the smoke-darkened air rent with the groans of the dying.

'He would never think—he could not be so cruel!' she gasps. 'He would not hazard the life that is so dear—'

'Hazard, my dear Mrs. Westray! He would be in no more danger among the belligerents than in the retirement of his own study. You never heard of a special correspondent coming to grief. They talk very big, and to read their letters one would suppose they rode shoulder to shoulder with the commanding officer; but it's my belief they sit quietly by a wood fire in some roadside inn near the scene of operations, and get their information hot and hot from small boys. Your small boy would go up to the cannon's mouth and look into it for sixpence. I shall be angry with myself if I have given you the slightest alarm. After all, Westray may have no idea of accepting the *Day Star* people's offer. All I know is, that the offer was made, and talked about at Mrs. Brandreth's. But no doubt he has refused it, or he would have told you.'

'Yes,' Editha says, slowly recovering composure; 'he would have told me. He never kept a secret from me in his life.'

'Ah, that's what all wives say,' thinks Lyndhurst; 'but I fancy I could tell you something about him that would astonish you for all that.'

He has given her an uncomfortable unsettled feeling about her absent husband, and that for the moment is enough; so he changes the subject, talks of the scenery, admires Priory and garden. Editha has forgotten her idea of offering him tea till he reminds her of her promise to introduce him to her sister.

'Miss Morcombe is fond of music, you told me?' he says.

'Passionately; and she hears so little good music. I shall be very pleased if you will play to her. There is a harmonium in her room—the best papa could get for her. Herr **Louis Engel** chose it. Will you come to Ruth's room and have some tea?'

'I shall be charmed.'

They go in together, and Ruth looks up from Jeremy Taylor's *Rule of Conscience*—she is a lover of the old divine, whose quaintness and classic lore have a curious charm for her—astonished at the appearance of a stranger.

'Mr. Lyndhurst, my sister. You have heard me talk of Mr. Lyndhurst, Ruth, one of Herman's old friends.'

The tea-table is ready. Editha takes off her hat, and seats herself before the old-fashioned silver urn, just as in the old days when Herman first came to the Priory. Something of the glow and freshness of untroubled youth has faded from her face since that happy time, but the face has gained in dignity and beauty. To Lyndhurst it looks like the face of a queen.

'My queen, at any rate,' he says to himself; 'my lady, whom to love is honour.'

He takes his place at her side presently—Herman's old place—and performs the small services of the tea-table, addressing his conversation chiefly to Ruth, whom he is desirous to conciliate. They would seem to have not an idea in common, this invalid recluse and the sin-dyed man of the world. Yet they get on wonderfully well. Ruth's book, in its old-fashioned tree-calf binding, has slipped from the silken coverlet at her knee to the carpet. Lyndhurst picks it up, glances at the title as he returns it, and begins to talk about the learned Jeremy, whose pages he knows as well as those of Balzac or Dumas fils, Feydeau or Flaubert, Heine or Spielhagen. A great reader Mr. Lyndhurst, in those midday hours which he gives to the repose of his body, and in the small hours sometimes, when he has made the idle experiment of going to bed soon after midnight. He has a shelf of his favourite books and a reading-lamp at the head of his bed, and takes down a volume of Heine or De Musset and reads himself into dreamland, when a man less careful of his own well-being would take a dose of chloral.

Mr. Lyndhurst sips his orange pekoe with an air of quiet enjoyment that bespeaks a placid soul refreshed by this pure and gentle society. It is strange how much he relishes the novelty of the situation. Mephistopheles drinking tea with Margaret and her mother could not be more out of place, could not carry the situation with a more consummate tact. After tea he goes to the harmonium at Editha's request, and plays Beethoven's Symphony in C minor, and then the 'Eroica,' and after that the 'Pastorale.' His listeners cannot have too much of that magnificent music. The harmonium peals out full organ notes, ripe and round, and fills the room with melody—melody which overflows into the corridor, where the Squire hears it on his way to that study or den where he reads the *Field* and the *Observer*, writes his letters, takes his afternoon nap, and occasionally goes into the mystery of accounts with his bailiff.

He looks in at the door, asking, 'Who have you got there, Ruth?' and thereupon renews his acquaintance with Hamilton Lyndhurst.

'I thought there was too much noise for our

little organist,' says Mr. Morcombe blandly. 'And so you have come down to try our sulphur or saline. Wonderful good they do you Londoners, I believe. Which are you taking—saline or sulphur?'

This is one of the conventional inquiries at Llandrysak. Mr. Lyndhurst looks embarrassed.

'My medical man advised sulphur,' he replies, with a lurking sparkle in those dark eyes of his, 'perhaps on the doctrine of signatures.'

'You must stop and dine with us of course. How did you come over?'

'I rode.'

'And you've put up your horse at the village inn? Why didn't you bring him here? He'd have been better taken care of.'

'No doubt. The village stable is certainly rather primitive, but I saw the corn put into his manger, and left him happy. I shall be too delighted to stop if I am not in the way.'

'In the way! We live so far out of the way that a visit from an intelligent stranger is the greatest luxury we can enjoy. How about this Ministry now? Will Gladstone bring in his bill next session, or retire upon his defeat, eh?' And the Squire begins to talk politics lustily, and speedily carries off his guest to see the gardens and the home-farm, but not before Lyndhurst has promised to return to Ruth's room after dinner, and play Mozart or Mendelssohn. He contrives to make himself agreeable to the Squire during that inspection of the premises; surveys the stables, which are Mr. Morcombe's especial pride, inspects all the horses, and pronounces on their various merits with an acumen which establishes him in their owner's good graces. No man can make a stronger or better impression in a given time than Hamilton Lyndhurst.

Mr. Petherick dines with them, and after dinner they all go up to Ruth's room to take their coffee and hear Mr. Lyndhurst play. It is quite a pleasant evening: the softly-lighted room; the two women, one a pale and fragile copy of the other's beauty, or say, rather, one a drawing in crayons, the other a painting in oils; the quaint old furniture and china harmoniously arranged, nothing crowded or ill assorted—make altogether a charming picture. It is ages since Hamilton Lyndhurst has felt himself the inmate of a home; and this is home; curiously different from the houses he visits in London, which have the air of being public places of entertainment, minus the moneytaker at the doors, and sometimes minus the amusement.

He leaves regretfully at the stroke of ten, and rides away in the clear summer moonlight, feeling as if he had been in Paradise. Unhappily the rose-hued light of an earthly Eden is too mild a fire to purify a sin-steeped soul like his, and he rides back to Llandrysak calmly meditative of evil, the solemn hills looking down at him, distant worlds shining upon him, the mystery of the universe around and about him, and affecting him no more deeply than it does the field-mouse, whose sharp beady eyes look warily out of its hole under the hedge yonder.

CHAPTER XIII.

'No settled senses of the world can match
The pleasure of that madness.'

Mr. Lyndhurst's groom rides over to Lochwithian before breakfast next morning, and Editha finds the first number of the *Connoisseur* beside her plate on the breakfast-table, packed in an official-looking vellum envelope, and sealed with Lyndhurst's monogram. He pretends to no ancient lineage, confesses frankly that his grandfather sold oranges in Houndsditch, and is above the petty pride of a purchased coat-of-arms.

Editha opens the packet with eager hands. The *Connoisseur* is a journal of gentlemanly aspect, printed on thick creamy-hued paper, in fair readable type, largely spaced, and with wide columns. *Chic* is the predominant characteristic of the new periodical. It abuses roundly, is outspoken, insolent even, but not snobbish or petty. It has a good-natured arrogance, a soldierly freedom of speech, and that delightful modern scepticism which may fairly be called unbelief in everything.

Editha turns with a glowing cheek to the poem ʼΑΝΑΓΚΗ, which occupies a place of honour in the middle of the paper; but that blush of wifely pride pales as she reads, and before she has finished the poem, she rises from the table to hide the tears of wounded feeling.

The verses are the complaint of a soul ill at ease; weariness, disappointment, unbelief, are expressed in every line. No happy husband, no Christian gentleman, could have thought these thoughts or written these words, Mrs. Westray tells herself. They are verses eminently calculated to take the town; for they breathe just that spirit of disappointment in the past and indifference about the future which is the dominant note of town life.

Editha looks at the signature through blinding tears. Yes, it is his name; he boldly signs this confession of no-faith. She has been his wife two years, and yet knows him so little that these verses come upon her like a revelation. Her love, her devotion, her unwearied thoughts of him and care for him, have been unsufficing for his happiness. He writes of himself as a disappointed man; a man for whom life and love have alike been failures. He writes of Fate and man's future like an infidel.

Could she but know exactly the truth about this unlucky little poem, which has cost her bitter tears, and brought her husband a handsome cheque, she would know that the verses were dashed off after a disagreeable interview with Mr. Standish the publisher, in which that gentleman complained of the result of Herman's last novel, and offered two hundred and fifty less for his next; she would know that Herman's spirit had been furthermore disturbed by a slashing criticism of his last play in the *Censor*, where he found himself stigmatised as the latest perverter of dramatic taste and poisoner of public morals, to say nothing of being condemned as an ignoramus, unacquainted with his own language, and unprovided with a dictionary.

Thus lashed to fury, his Muse had raised her crest somewhere in the small hours, shaken her tresses savagely, like another Medusa, and hit out against Fate : **Fate** meaning at this moment a decline of two hundred and fifty pounds in the market price of a three-volume novel and the small carpings of an anonymous critic.

Unhappily Editha takes the matter in sober seriousness, weighs every word, ponders every latent meaning, and is miserable. She locks up the paper as if it were a guilty secret. Not for worlds would she have those dreadful verses read by Ruth. She writes to her husband in the hour between breakfast and church time; a long piteous letter, telling him how shocked and grieved she has been by sentiments which seem to her like a new language from his pen, asking him about the *Day Star's* offer, and if he had ever been *so cruel* as to think for one moment of going to the scene of war; and finally imploring him to come down to Lochwithian, if it were only for a few days' rest for himself, or for that much lesser reason—only to make her happy.

'You thought very little of coming backwards and forwards when we were engaged,' she adds, with gentle reproachfulness. 'Have I less claim upon you now I am your wife, and when our child is just old enough to ask in his baby-language why you are not here?'

She is not a little surprised to see Mr. Lyndhurst stroll into the garden an hour after luncheon on this summer Sunday. She is carrying her boy round to look at the roses, which he examines critically with big round blue eyes, and sniffs daintily with a small 'tip-tilted' nose. She had not heard the Squire's hospitable invitation to his new acquaintance last night, and had no idea that Mr. Lyndhurst was to eat his Sabbath dinner at the Priory.

'I hope you won't think me a tremendous nuisance, Mrs. Westray,' he says apologetically. 'Your father was good enough to ask me to drive over this afternoon, and I could not refuse such a tempting offer. Llandrysak on Sunday is the abomination of desolation. The bell of the little Anglican church sounds like the stroke of a toasting-fork upon a frying-pan; the Independent chapel tinkles and jangles all the morning. The Independents begin to howl hymns at ten; the Anglicans intone at half-past. You can hear both melodious sounds far away across the common in the silence of the place. When Slingsby Edwards has finished his sermon, his flock troops off to the Anglicans to make a finish. Shows a mind unfettered by sectarianism, doesn't it ?'

Editha's grave looks reprove this jesting with sacred things; so Mr. Lyndhurst turns his attention to the baby. Praise a woman's child, or horse, or dog, and you find the surest short cut to her favour. The child inclines to Hamilton at once, as four-footed animals incline to him, perhaps because he is big, powerful, and débonnaire, and has a surface benignity which attracts unreasoning creatures.

The Squire appears presently, returning from his farm, in a straw hat, and with a Sunday-afternoon listlessness of gait and manner; and they all wander about the gardens, and down through the orchard to the ruins, Mr. Lyndhurst carrying the baby on his shoulder, and feeling himself quite a domestic character. They dawdle about, looking at the rugged old stone walls, threaded with pale spleenwort and gray mosses, and speculating upon the plan of nave and aisles, transept and apse, sacristy and lady chapel. They stroll down to the river—that placid trout stream which was wont to flow through the Priory kitchen. There bloom the forget-me-nots, which Herman and Editha plucked together three years ago in the untroubled morning of their love. How well she remembers that day and the new dreams it brought her, the faint vague hopes which she tried to shut out of her mind, fearing a new influence which might come between her and Ruth! Now, Ruth is only second in her life, tenderly beloved still, but never again the first.

'I might have been happier if I had been true to Ruth,' she thinks sadly, as her father and Mr. Lyndhurst stroll on a little in advance of her, talking politics, the baby deliciously content with his lofty perch, looking down at his mother as she slowly follows, full of thought.

If she had been true to Ruth, if she had made up her mind at once and for ever to remain unmarried for love of Ruth, how much care, how many a pain she might have missed! It would have been a hard thing to refuse that ardent lover, a hard thing to reject the sweet responsibility of wifehood; but once the sacrifice made, how easy all the rest of life! How simple, how single her duty as Ruth's nurse and consoler! how complicated, how difficult as Herman's wife! He has committed to her the custody of his days, the guardianship of his fame; and how little she has done for either! She has trebled the cost of his existence, and has not succeeded in making his home happy, since he goes elsewhere in search of amusement. Upon his art she has exercised no influence whatever, since the last page he has published proves that in thought and opinion they two, husband and wife, are wide as the poles asunder. Her reverence for things that are holy, her deep and fervent faith, have had no more effect upon his way of looking at life than if he had spent the last two years of his existence among South-Sea Islanders.

They dine at six, and when the Squire and his guest return to the drawing-room after dinner, Editha has gone to church; whereby Mr. Lyndhurst finds the next two hours hang somewhat heavily on hand. Mr. Morcombe has shown him the stables and the home-farm. He has seen the ruins—the garden. There is really nothing more for him to see at Lochwithian, except the inexhaustible hills. The Squire's conversation waxes monotonous. They go out into the garden, and smoke their cigars amidst the odours of roses and honeysuckle. Lyndhurst looks at the church-window, whence shines the faint gleam of the pulpit-candles, and wonders how much longer the service is to last. Anon comes the sound of the organ, village voices singing an evening hymn, and then the little congregation comes slowly out of the gray gothic porch, and presently Mr. Lyndhurst hears the click of the garden-gate, which announces Editha's return. She must pass them on her way to the house.

'Good-night, papa,' she says. 'I am going to Ruth's room, and I don't think I shall come downstairs again unless you want me. Good-night, Mr. Lyndhurst.'

'Out of sorts, pet?' asks the Squire, scrutinising her after his good-night kiss. 'You are looking pale. No bad news from Westray, is there?'

'No, papa; I've a headache, that's all.'

'Thunder in the air, no doubt. Good-night dear; go and rest.'

And so, after a friendly good-night to Mr. Lyndhurst, Editha leaves them, and the Squire and his guest go down to the gate to waylay Parson Petherick, who comes in to smoke a cigar with them after his day's long labour.

That unhappy look of Editha's haunts Hamilton Lyndhurst as he drives back to Llandrysak.

'She has begun to doubt him,' he thinks. 'That sceptical poem has made her miserable. If she is so wretched because he has shown himself something less holy than the saint she has made him, what will she suffer when she knows more? When she knows that the moth has flown back to the flame that lured him years ago, and that his wings are singed by the old fire?'

END OF VOL. II.

www.ingramcontent.com/pod-product-compliance
Lightning Source LLC
Chambersburg PA
CBHW032100220426
43664CB00008B/1080